The Prophets

GOD'S WORD TODAY III

A New Study Guide to the Bible

Emil A. Wcela

The Prophets

God's Spokesmen through the Years

Suggestions for Reflection
by Sr. Jeanne Monahan O.P.

PUEBLO PUBLISHING COMPANY
NEW YORK

Nihil Obstat: *Daniel V. Flynn, J.C.D.*
Censor Librorum

Imprimatur: *Joseph T. O'Keefe*
Vicar General
Archdiocese of New York
January 5, 1980

Design: *Frank Kacmarcik*

ISBN: 0-916134-31-8

Printed in the United States of America

To my family

to my mother, to Joseph, Barbara, Ronald, Regina and Diane

to the memory of my father and Joseph, Jr., whom we hope to join one day in God's presence

CONTENTS

PREFACE

Interest in the Scriptures continues to grow. Men and women individually and in groups read, reflect on, discuss, pray from the Bible. I have taught, led, participated in such groups. This participation has convinced me that, despite all the worthwhile material on the Bible already available, there are still gaps to be filled for those people who truly care about the Bible but have had little or no preparation to extract its riches.

Several excellent guides to the Bible exist in the format of booklet series in which each volume provides commentary and explanation on a separate book of the Bible. However, for someone becoming acquainted with the Bible, to work through each book one by one can be a formidable task.

Other books focus on themes and main ideas distilled from the whole Bible. As valuable as such theologies and overall views are, there is still a need for a familiarity with the *text* of the Bible itself.

In this series, substantial portions of the Scriptures—extensive enough to convey style, language, tone—are the indispensable starting point. Essential background and explanation are provided and the lasting import of the text is suggested. Possibilities for individual or group reflection are offered.

When the reader has completed this series, he will have encountered many themes and main ideas, and this through a selected and guided reading of the text itself. This overall view can be filled in by further study of the individual books of the Bible.

The general plan emerges from a listing of the titles in this series. It is my strong recommendation that anyone using the series begin with Volume I. If the principles presented there are grasped, the spadework will be done for understanding what follows.

Vol. I:	THE BIBLE: What it is and how it developed.
Vol. II:	BASIC BELIEFS IN GENESIS AND EXODUS
Vol. III:	THE PROPHETS: God's spokesmen through the years.
Vol. IV:	THE STORY OF ISRAEL: God's people through the years.
Vol. V:	JESUS, HIS WORD AND WORK: The gospels of Matthew, Mark and Luke.
Vol. VI:	THE GOSPEL OF JOHN
Vol. VII:	PAUL THE PASTOR: His teaching in the First Letter to the Corinthians.
Vol. VIII:	PAUL THE THEOLOGIAN: His teaching in the Letter to the Romans.

"Indeed, God's word is living and effective, sharper than any two-edged sword. It penetrates and divides soul and spirit, joints and marrow; it judges the reflections and thoughts of the heart" (Hebrews 4.12).

Emil A. Wcela
Series Editor

FOREWORD

This is the last of the books that I am scheduled to write in this series. Over the years that the project has been in the planning and through publication, many people have offered support, encouragement, advice. I especially wish to express my gratitude to my former colleagues on the faculty of the Seminary of the Immaculate Conception, Huntington, New York, and to the students preparing for priesthood and other ministries there with whom I have studied the Scriptures. A special word of thanks is due to Sister Jeanne Monahan whose suggestions and study questions opened up many new insights and to Father George Denzer who over the years has taught me more than I can say about God's Word and who read each of the manuscripts and offered very valuable comments and corrections.

SOME PROPHETS

	Dates	*Preached to*
Elijah	c. 850	Israel
Amos	c. 750	Israel
Hosea	c. 745	Israel
721	The conquest of Israel by the Assyrians The end of the northern kingdom	
Isaiah	c. 740-700	Judah
Jeremiah	c. 627-587	Judah
Ezekiel	c. 593-573	Judah and the exiles
587	The conquest of Judah by the Babylonians The destruction of Jerusalem and the Temple The exile	
Second Isaiah	c. 550-540	The exiles
538	The Persian king, Cyrus, allows the Jewish exiles to return home	

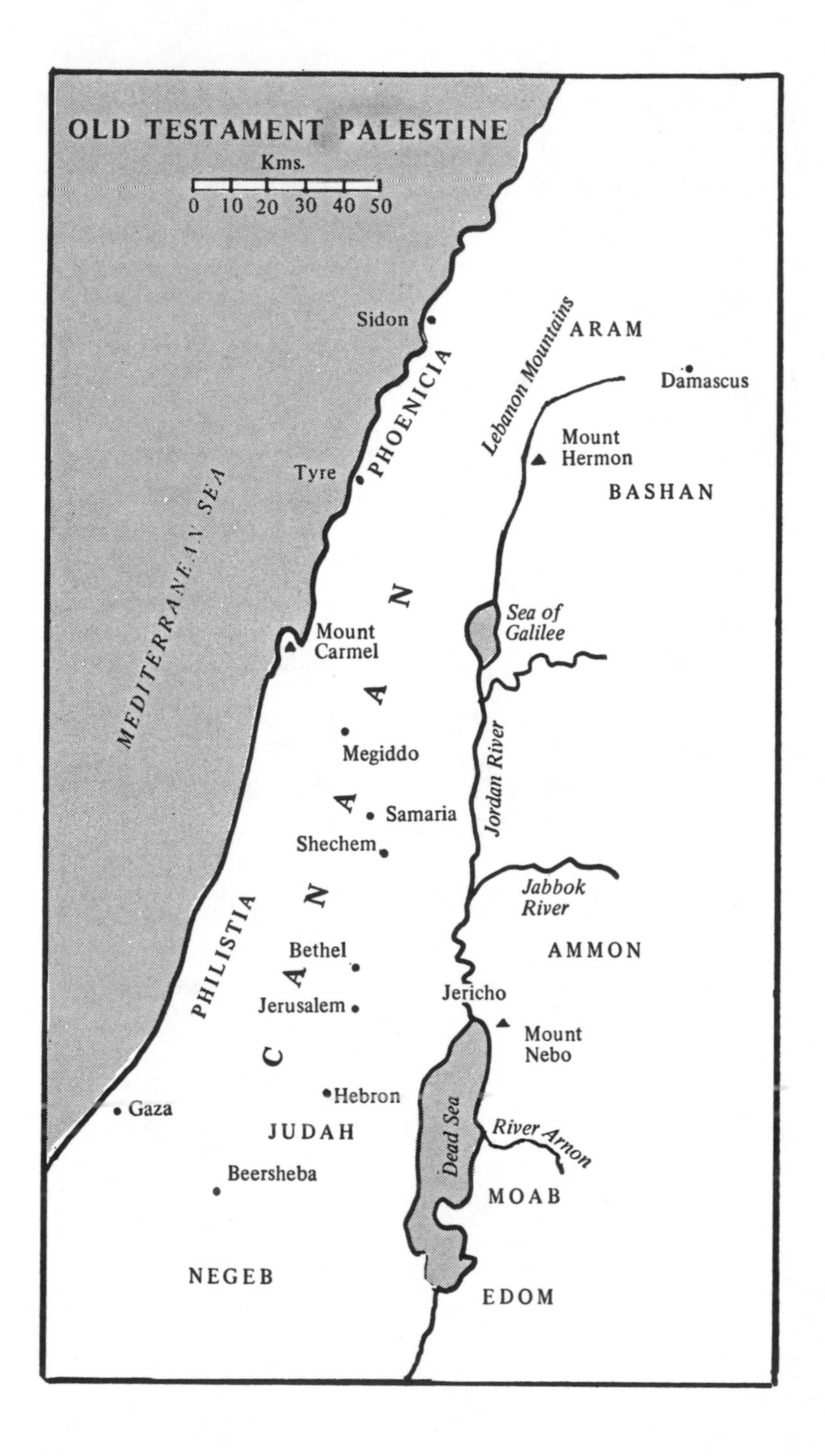
OLD TESTAMENT PALESTINE
Kms.
0 10 20 30 40 50
MEDITERRANEAN SEA
Sidon
ARAM
Lebanon Mountains
PHOENICIA
Damascus
Mount
Hermon
Tyre
BASHAN
C A N A A N
Sea of
Galilee
Mount
Carmel
Megiddo
Jordan River
Samaria
Shechem
Jabbok
River
PHILISTIA
Bethel
AMMON
Jericho
Jerusalem
Mount
Nebo
Hebron
Gaza
JUDAH
Dead Sea
River Arnon
Beersheba
MOAB
NEGEB
EDOM

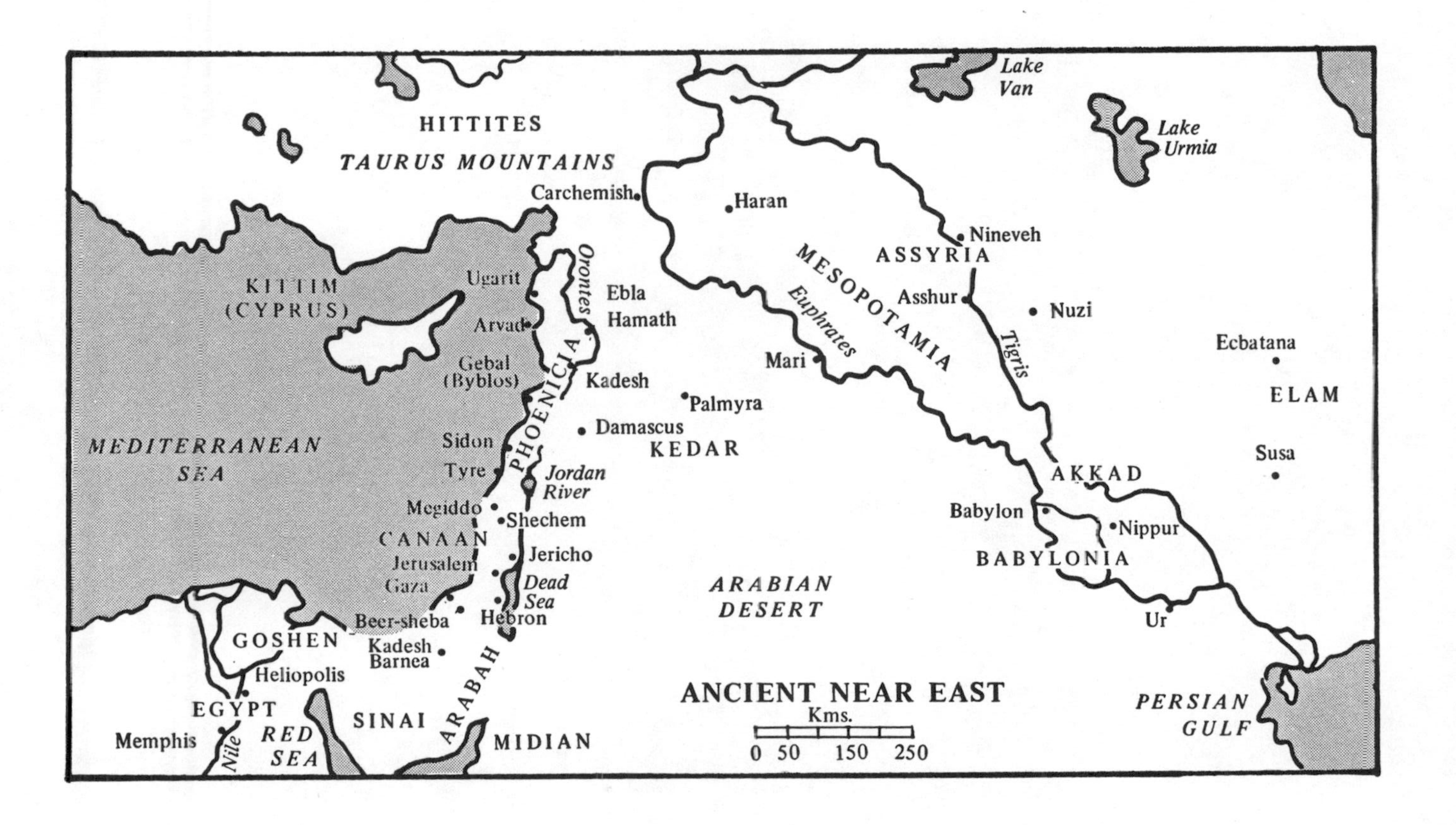
ANCIENT NEAR EAST
Kms.
0 50 150 250
HITTITES
TAURUS MOUNTAINS
Carchemish
Haran
Lake Van
Lake Urmia
Nineveh
ASSYRIA
MESOPOTAMIA
Asshur
Nuzi
Euphrates
Tigris
Mari
Ecbatana
ELAM
Susa
KITTIM (CYPRUS)
Ugarit
Arvad
Gebal (Byblos)
Orontes
Ebla
Hamath
Kadesh
Palmyra
Damascus
KEDAR
PHOENICIA
MEDITERRANEAN SEA
Sidon
Tyre
Jordan River
Megiddo
Shechem
CANAAN
Jericho
Jerusalem
Gaza
Dead Sea
Beer-sheba
Hebron
GOSHEN
Kadesh Barnea
Heliopolis
EGYPT
Memphis
Nile
RED SEA
SINAI
ARABAH
MIDIAN
ARABIAN DESERT
AKKAD
Babylon
Nippur
BABYLONIA
Ur
PERSIAN GULF

CHAPTER I

WHAT IS A PROPHET?

LIVING WITH PROPHETS

The word, "prophet," has come into its own in our day. As the world and the church have changed, individuals have emerged who have taken strong public stands for and against much of what is going on around us.

Pope John XXIII has often been called a "prophet" because of his attempt to move the church more fully into dialogue with the world.

Others believe that the church should not be moving into dialogue but into confrontation with most of what is happening. Movements in the United States and Europe look to the past, to what are interpreted as perennial characteristics of the church, its ritual, its organization. These movements have their leaders, people looked upon as "prophets," proclaiming their own particular, sometimes peculiar, message. The controversy concerning Archbishop Lefebvre and his associates is an example of this kind of movement taken to extremes.

The name, "prophet," has also been applied to a wide range of people in other activities. Several years ago, some called the Berrigan brothers "prophets" for their anti-Vietnam-war stance. Mother Teresa of India is often referred to as a "prophet" because of the challenge of her simple Christian life and message of love and service.

From these few examples, it is clear that the term, "prophet," is rather broadly used. And I haven't even mentioned the designation of those who try to foretell the future as "prophets."

For us in a religious context, the word generally communicates the image of someone fired by a new spirit, marching to a different drum even in the face of personal hazard.

Who is and who is not truly a prophet is not always immediately obvious.

For example, if it was prophetic to try to relate church to world, to deepen the understanding and dialogue between church and world, then it cannot also be prophetic to say that the church is static and fixed and cannot change in any way if it is to fulfill its mission. On the other hand, if it is prophetic to challenge certain directions that do not seem correct, then it cannot also be prophetic to say in an unqualified way, "we're all ok."

PROPHECY AS A COMMON EXPERIENCE

The study of religions over the centuries shows a phenomenon common to all which can be given the name, "prophecy," and helps us to define "prophet" more precisely. Common denominators emerge.

1. The prophet is convinced that he or she is in contact with the world of the gods or God.

2. The prophet is convinced of a call to communicate the mysteries of that divine world.

3. The prophet is convinced that his or her message and the impulse to share that message with others do not come from personal whim but from a divine push to do so.

I emphasize again that we are not yet speaking of the truth or falsity of a prophet's message, only of what experience shows to be a set of personal convictions that seem to characterize a particular group of people within religious experience.

PROPHETS OUTSIDE THE BIBLE

Some 1800 years before Christ, there was an important city on the Euphrates River called Mari. About forty years ago, archeologists began to sift through the remains of the city. Among the finds were over 20,000 rectangular tablets of baked clay, the common writing material. On these tablets were inscribed the correspondence of the kings and records pertaining to business and religion. About twenty-three of these tablets contain what are presented as messages from the gods communicated through prophets. Most of the messages are about the king, his safety, the threat of rebellion against him, the possibility of military successes. The information comes through a person who has been in some way influenced by a god or goddess.

Greek authors of about 500 B.C. tell us that they were well acquainted with prophets. In fact the word, prophet, comes from a Greek word, *prophetes,* which means "one who speaks for another," "an interpreter." The prophet or prophetess was one through whom the god communicated a message. Somehow the god took possession of the prophet and while in this state, the prophet spoke in the god's name.

The history of Christianity reveals many individuals who believed that Jesus was speaking through them. St. Bridget of Sweden in the fourteenth century was conscious of such a relationship with Jesus. On one occasion, she perceived that she had been commanded by Jesus to go to Rome and give the Pope and the Emperor a message from him.

DEFINITION OF A PROPHET

Johannes Lindblom, who has written a careful and thorough work on prophecy called *Prophecy in Ancient Israel,* comes to the following definition after considering the phenomenon in various religions through history.

"A prophet may be characterized as a person who, because he is conscious of having been specially chosen and called, feels forced to perform actions and proclaim ideas which, in a mental state of intense inspiration or real ecstasy, have been indicated to him in the form of divine revelations."

EARLY PROPHETS IN THE BIBLE

Please read: 1 Samuel 10.5-13; 19.22-24

The tradition that there are prophets, special people who speak for Yahweh, is constant through the Hebrew Scriptures. The common Hebrew word for prophet is *nabi.* We can best understand the early history of these people by a survey of some of the Old Testament passages which tell about them.

Both passages indicated above are set in a time framework about 1020 years before Christ. The holy man, Samuel, is himself a prophet. Yahweh had revealed to him, "At this time tomorrow I will send you a man from the land of Benjamin whom you are to anoint as commander of my people Israel. He shall save my people from the clutches of the Philistines, for I have witnessed their misery and accepted their cry for help" (1 Samuel 9.16). The man whom Samuel is to make commander is Saul. When Samuel meets Saul, he tells him that as a sign that Yahweh has really chosen him for a special work, Saul will "meet a band of prophets, in a prophetic state, coming down from the high place preceded by lyres, tambourines, flutes and harps. The spirit of the LORD will rush upon you, and you will join them in their prophetic state and will be changed into another man." All this happens.

There are a number of things that this passage tells us about prophets.

First, there is a band of them. These particular prophets have formed an association.

Then, they are "in a prophetic state," which has to mean some unusual state of mind and activity.

Still further, they are accompanied by people playing on musical instruments. This suggests that the music has something to do with their state of mind.

Finally, Saul is told that when the "spirit of the LORD" comes upon him, he will "join them in their prophetic state and will be changed into another man." At this stage, prophecy could involve some change in personality. This change can best be described as ecstasy, a situation in which the prophet seems to be taken over by another force or being. The Israelites believed that their true prophets were possessed by the spirit of Yahweh.

That prophecy at this time could include a change in behavior is suggested again in 19.18-24. Saul has sent some of his men to arrest David who was staying with Samuel. When Saul's men came to where Samuel and David were staying, "they saw the band of prophets, presided over by Samuel, in a prophetic frenzy (and) they too fell into the prophetic state." When Saul himself arrived, "the spirit of God came upon him also, and he continued in a prophetic condition." In this condition, "he stripped himself of his garments and he, too, remained in the prophetic state."

Here prophecy is associated with an apparent take-over of personality by God. When this happens, the prophet seems to have no control over his actions. Notice also that there is once again a band of prophets and they are under the leadership of Samuel. What they say or the purpose of their ecstatic state is still not clear from these passages.

ELIJAH

Please read: 1 Kings 17–19, 21; 2 Kings 2

The books of Kings provide more detailed sketches of two ninth century B.C. prophets, Elijah and Elisha.

Elijah appears during the reign of Ahab, a king of Israel, the northern kingdom (874-53). This king had married a princess from the coastal city of Tyre. She was a devotee of Baal, the god of her own kingdom. As the wife of the king of Israel, she not only fostered the religion of her god but persecuted those who remained faithful to Israel's God, Yahweh. The text sums up the situation in these words of Elijah: "the Israelites have forsaken your covenant, torn down your altars, and put your prophets to the sword. I alone am left, and they seek to take my life" (19.10).

Elijah emerges as the heart of the resistance among faithful Israelites to the false religion being forced on them by a foreign queen.

ELIJAH AND BAAL

Chapter 17 contains legendary stories about Elijah treasured by his followers much as the members of religious communities value the recollections and legends that grow up around their founders and holy persons. For example, a collection of stories about St. Francis known as the "Little Flowers" includes a legend about a fierce wolf which terrorized the town of Gubbio, attacking both people and animals. Francis met the wolf, tamed it and the wolf thereafter became the village pet.

Here, one story tells how ravens brought food for Elijah while he was in hiding. Another tells how, during a drought that Elijah had predicted, he miraculously provided food for a widow and her son. When a boy fell sick and died, Elijah raised him to life.

The key incident in the Elijah story is in 18.20-40. At stake is the direction that the Israelites should take. Should they remain faithful to Yahweh, the God who brought them through the desert and into the promised land? Or should they accept the god of the land in which they have settled. The local god, Baal, is a god of fertility and growth. Now that they are becoming farmers and owners of flocks, ought they not turn to a god whose field of operation seems to be more in line with their present needs than the God of their fathers? In other words, isn't it time for some updating?

The story describes a contest that Elijah arranges to let Yahweh and Baal show the extent of their power. Elijah goes into enemy territory. The contest is to take place on Mt. Carmel, sacred to Canaanite religion. What actually happened can no longer be determined. The passage tells that the contest revolved around fire from heaven lighting a sacrifice prepared on the mountain.

Wood is prepared. A slaughtered bull is laid on it. The prophets of Baal are told by Elijah to invite their god to set the wood on fire. While they dance around the altar and call upon Baal, Elijah taunts them. "Call louder, for he is a god and may be meditating, or may have retired, or may be on a journey. Perhaps he is asleep and must be awakened."

Nothing happens even when the prophets of Baal do call louder and go through their bloody custom of slashing themselves with knives. Then Elijah prepares his wood and sacrificial bull and, to make things more difficult, pours water over the wood. In contrast to the frenzied activity of his opponents, Elijah, with quiet dignity, calls on the God of Israel to light the sacrificial fire.

Yahweh responds. Fire from heaven consumes the sacrifices. The people acknowledge Yahweh as God. Elijah executes the prophets of Baal.

It was Elijah's role to call the people back to Yahweh in the face of terrible apostasy. They would have relegated Yahweh to their past and been willing to deny his place in their present life.

ELIJAH, YAHWEH AND SOCIAL JUSTICE

Chapter 21 gives another important insight into the role of the prophet.

Ahab, by now established as a fickle and faithless king, has designs on a vineyard next to his palace. He offers the owner, Naboth, a better vineyard elsewhere or money.

The deal sounds very attractive. The problem is that the land is Naboth's "ancestral heritage."

Their own land was something sacred for the Israelites. It represented their stake in the land Yahweh had promised. As such, its value went far beyond the income it might provide or the money for which it might be sold. For these reasons, Naboth refuses to part with his land.

Ahab's wife notices the angry pouting of her husband. The infamous but resourceful Jezebel comes up with a solution to his problem.

A phony trial against Naboth is staged and culminates in his execution. Ahab is then free to take over the vineyard.

However, Ahab has not counted on the avenging figure of Elijah. Elijah confronts Ahab with the evil of what he has done and foretells that, as punishment for the crime, the family of Ahab will be wiped out.

What Elijah stands for is the authentic view of the role of the king in Israel. In other parts of the Near East, the king was above the law, able to do pretty much as he pleased. This was not so in Israel. The king was not king to suit his own purposes. Nor was he above the law which ruled the life of the people and was accepted as Yahweh's way.

The king was to be an instrument of Yahweh and his purposes for Israel and the world. Ahab had failed in this. He tried to use kingship to further personal ambitions. All Israelites were equal because all were members of the people chosen by Yahweh. Ahab had abused this relationship by his manipulation of events to bring about the death of a fellow Israelite and the royal confiscation of his heritage.

Elijah as prophet became the spokesman for God's wrath against such perversity and injustice.

EARLY PROPHETS: SUMMARY

When the passages we have read are put together with all the other information about Israel's prophets in the period from about the year 1000 to the year 750, the result is a complex picture.

The following brief comments would seem to sum up the main elements of the developing prophetic movement in Israel.

1. The early prophets were convinced that they had been given insights into the workings of Yahweh.

2. Often, this elevated knowledge came while the prophet was in a state of ecstasy. This ecstasy could be induced by music and dancing. However, ecstasy was not always a preliminary to prophecy.

3. Some prophets lived a community life, often under the leadership of some esteemed individual such as Samuel or Elisha. However, this community life was not absolutely essential because other prophets lived in customary home and family situations.

4. Prophets sometimes adopted visible signs of what they were. They might wear animal skins, or mark a cross-shaped design on their foreheads, or have their hair cut in a kind of tonsure.

5. Prophets sometimes lived close by the places sacred to Israel. When pilgrims came to visit these shrines, they would meet the prophets.

6. When kingship became accepted as a regular institution, the kings attached groups of prophets to their courts. These were supported by the king. Their function was to be spokesmen for Yahweh to the king. As the king became involved in his various projects, these prophets were to let him know what Yahweh thought of it all. Of course, in this situation it was not unexpected that somehow Yahweh's word through these prophets was most often exactly what the kings wanted to hear.

7. The role of the prophets varied. Their primary function was to speak in Yahweh's name. They were spokesmen for Yahweh, whether to the nation or to individuals. Sometimes they functioned at the sanctuaries when crowds of people came to celebrate feasts in honor of Yahweh.

This speaking in Yahweh's name meant that at their best, the prophets were defenders of true faith in Yahweh. They would condemn false steps Israel might be taking in working out its relationship with Yahweh. They might encourage a certain way of life or direction in which Israel ought to move. They might defend moral or social values. At times, they might condemn the king for his abuse of power. Elijah did this. So did Nathan. David had arranged things so that the husband of a woman he lusted for would be killed in battle. David could then legitimate his affair with the woman, Bathsheba, by marrying her. Nathan confronted David with what he had done and threatened him with Yahweh's punishment.

In the northern kingdom of Israel, the prophets seem to have played an active role in politics. In the southern kingdom of Judah, it was accepted principle that the family of David was to be the ruling family. This was not so in the north. There was no understanding that son would succeed father. This left the way open to intrigue and assassination. Some prophets become involved in these machinations, especially if they feel that the king in possession has not been faithful to Yahweh.

All in all, the prophet was a familiar figure during this period. He was respected and feared by king and commoner alike. It was recognized that he was in some special relationship with Yahweh and could bring good or evil.

PRIMITIVE PROPHETS AND CLASSICAL PROPHETS

Thus far we have been reading about the early years of prophecy in Israel. We have descriptions of prophets and what they did. We have some stories about the way they lived and what they said. But for none of these prophets do we have a collection of the words they spoke in Yahweh's name.

In the next chapter, and for the rest of the book, we shall be dealing with a different situation. We shall be reading the words of the prophets, at least some of whose sayings were preserved.

This is an important difference between the so-called "primitive prophets" and the "classical prophets." The term "classical prophet" indicates one whose words spoken in Yahweh's name have been handed on to us.

As our reading progresses, we shall see that there are other significant differences between the "primitive" and "classical" prophets.

SUGGESTIONS FOR REFLECTION

1. In reading through the common denominators descriptive of prophets (page 2), think of persons in public life or your own local sphere who seem to be led by these three aspects of experience.

2. The prophets were truly the "conscience of Israel" in the ways they spoke in Yahweh's name in the face of injustice, infidelity, and idolatry–by the nation and by individuals. They also gave direction in ways that Israel should live and move as a people. What personal qualities did such a role demand? Why is it difficult today for someone to be a "conscience for the people" morally or socially? What would such a role demand of an individual in terms of relationship to God and life values and style?

3. Unique in the heritage of Israel were the concepts of sacredness of their own land, faithful worship of one God only, king as Yahweh's servant and instrument, equality of persons, and power to be used only for Yahweh's purposes. Show how the early prophets were Yahweh's spokesmen in preserving these values.

4. Prophets were familiar figures in the primitive age. "They were respected and feared by king and commoner alike." Is this the same condition today? Why? Why not?

5. Would you personally like to be a prophet? Like to have a prophet as your best friend or member of your family? Explain your reasons.

CHAPTER II

AMOS AND THE JUDGMENT OF GOD ON ALL PEOPLE

From the first chapter, it should be clear that the main work of a prophet in Israel was not to foretell the future but to speak in the name of Yahweh to his people. Of course, this often included insights into the future.

As we encounter representative prophets, it will be important to consider the following points:

1. The time and circumstances during which the prophet preached.
2. The prophet himself.
3. The prophetic call. Each prophet is aware of some experience or some situation in which he received a call to do Yahweh's work. Very often the prophet gives an account of his call. A careful study of this "call story" generally reveals the chief points and the special characteristics of his message.
4. A selection of texts representative of the prophet's message.

We are leaving aside a number of important issues for now. How did the prophet get his message? What was his state of mind? How was his message preserved, etc.

These issues will be treated with more appreciation after we have become acquainted with two prophets, Amos and Hosea.

AMOS, HIS TIMES

Please read: Amos 1.1

Amos appeared on the scene about the year 750 B.C. This was a time of prosperity for the people of the twin kingdoms of Judah and Israel. A king named Jeroboam II ruled in the northern kingdom of Israel. His counterpart in the southern kingdom, Judah, was Uzziah. Each of these kings enjoyed a long reign, from roughly 780 to about 740 B.C. During this time, the double kingdom of Israel and Judah had almost the territory and importance of the golden days of David and Solomon. Both kings expanded their control into the lands around them. Building and rebuilding projects were inaugurated. Trade and commerce flourished.

On the other hand, decay was eating away at the welfare of the people and the nation. This corruption showed itself especially in two areas of life.

1. *religious mediocrity*

Belief in Yahweh was for many a mere formality. The usual religious rituals were carried out but they had no impact on daily life. Almost as a matter of course, this lack of fervor tolerated and encouraged the wholesale transfer from pagan religions of attitudes and practices destructive to the religion of Yahweh.

2. *sharp class distinctions*

The growth in trade and commerce fostered the emergence of a wealthy class. In the Israelite ideal, all were equal because each person was one of God's chosen people. This equality crumbled as many of the rich oppressed and extorted from the poor to build up their own wealth.

AMOS HIMSELF

Please read: 1.1-2; 7.10-17

Most of the prophets, Amos included, tell us very little about themselves. This is because their chief concern is not themselves but the word of Yahweh which was being revealed through them.

The book of Amos tells us that Amos was a "shepherd from Tekoa." Amos' home was in the rough, mountainous country about ten miles south of Jerusalem. He was a man of the kingdom of Judah. However, his message was delivered in the northern kingdom of Israel.

Amos refers to himself as a "shepherd and a dresser of sycamores."

Because an unusual Hebrew word is used for "shepherd," it is not certain whether Amos was a rugged, poor hired man who cared for the flocks of others, or whether he was wealthy enough to own sheep and goats of his own. In either case, he spent weeks on end with the flocks in the barren lands that were suited only for grazing.

The sycamore tree produces a small fruit which was gathered and eaten especially by poor people. The fruit has to be punctured while it is maturing if it is to grow to any respectable size. Amos says that this was a seasonal job for him as a "dresser of sycamores."

Amos clashed with the priest at the shrine of Bethel. There were two national sanctuaries to Yahweh in the northern kingdom, one on the northern boundary at Dan and the other in the south at Bethel. Here Amos preached as the people streamed in on their pilgrimages. Amaziah, the priest in charge, reported to the king of Israel that Amos was voicing a harsh message of destruction and punishment for the king and his people. Obviously, neither king nor people took kindly to this strange figure speaking his uncomfortable words in their holy place.

Amaziah ordered Amos to go to the land of Judah from where he had come and do his prophesying there.

Amos answered that he could not be silenced. He was not a "professional" prophet, one of the group officially attached to the shrine. Rather he had received a special call from Yahweh himself to speak in his name.

Because Amaziah would not listen to the warning Yahweh was giving through Amos, he would see his sons and daughters slaughtered by an invading army and his wife made a prostitute for these invaders. His own land would be taken away from him and he himself would die in exile, as would many others in the kingdom of Israel.

THE CALL OF AMOS

Please read: 1.2; 3.3-8; 7.1-9; 8.1-3; 9.1-6

These passages convey Amos' sense of what he was about.

What he is communicating is Yahweh's word. The God who is present in the Temple on Mt. Zion in Jerusalem will "roar." His word, ignored by so many, will have such power that the fields in which shepherds pasture their flocks will dry up. Even Mt. Carmel, proverbial for fertility and rich vegetation, will wither. The word that Amos must speak will have devastating effects on man and nature.

In 3.3-8, Amos tries to communicate how helpless he himself is in the face of God's word which burns within him. Nothing happens without a cause. Two people do not walk together unless they have arrived at some meeting of minds. A lion does not roar unless it has found prey. A bird does not get caught in a trap unless something has lured it there. And when the trumpet sounds the alarm, the dwellers in the city become frightened. There is a reason for everything.

When a prophet speaks, an irresistible power is moving him. God is speaking!

"Indeed, the Lord GOD does nothing
without revealing his plan
to his servants, the prophets."

In 7.1-9, Amos recounts a series of visions. Possibly these are Amos' description of his call experience.

First, Amos sees a locust swarm in a devastating attack on the farmlands. The first crop, taken by the king as a tax, had been harvested. Now the second crop on which the people depended for their needs was beginning to grow. If the locusts devoured this crop, the people would have nothing. Amos asks God to hold off this plague. God, in his mercy, responds to Amos' prayer. Then Amos sees a great fire or drought devouring the land. Again, Amos intercedes with God to withdraw this threat to the life of his people. And again, God agrees.

In the third vision, Amos sees Yahweh standing by a wall. Yahweh drops a plumb line along the wall. The line reveals that the wall is grossly out of line. Yahweh says that it is just so with his people. He has no choice but to bring destruction upon them. This time, Amos perceives all too clearly the corruption of the people. He remains silent, making no plea for them.

In 8.1-3, Amos describes seeing a basket of ripe fruit, in Hebrew *qayis.* A play on words suggests the Hebrew word *qes,* meaning "end." The time is *ripe* for Yahweh to *end* his relationship with Israel. Their sins are such that he can forgive them no longer. They are bringing disaster on themselves.

The last vision is in 9.1-6. Amos is with the crowds gathered at the shrine of Bethel. While they celebrate in a festive spirit, Amos alone sees the God they pretend to worship standing beside the altar. His words are frightening. The devastation of war will overwhelm the people. None will escape, no matter where they flee. Yahweh will no longer tolerate the evil in his people.

YAHWEH, UNIVERSAL JUDGE OF EVIL DEEDS

Please read: 1.1–2.16

Yahweh's concern is not limited to the life of Israel and Judah. He is God whose power and will commands all nations. Amos denounces the crimes of six neighbors of Israel: Aram, Philistia, Tyre, Edom, Ammon and Moab. Each condemnation follows the same form: an introductory accusation, the details of the crime, the punishment to be meted out.

The expression, "for the three crimes and for four," is an ancient poetic device. A line of poetry moves forward by mentioning a number and then increasing it by one. That the numbers chosen are three and four very likely has to do with the fact that they add up to seven. Seven for the Israelites was a number of perfection. The nations are being condemned because their crimes have reached the peak of evil. They are "perfectly" evil. In each case, what calls for punishment is a crime against humanity.

Literally or figuratively, the people of Aram had dragged heavy sleds over the bodies of the people of Gilead whom they defeated in war (1.3). The people of Philistia were selling into slavery captives taken in war (1.6). Tyre was guilty of the same crime (1.9). The people of Edom pursued their wars with a fierce and unrelenting intensity, allowing no mercy (1.11). The Ammonites showed their brutishness by ripping open pregnant women captured in an expedition into a nearby region (1.13). The Moabites pursued an enemy king even beyond the grave, digging up and burning his bones (2.1).

Yahweh is not only the God of Israel. He is a God who remembers the horrors that any group perpetrates on any other group. Not only is false worship and religious malpractice an abomination to him but so also is what people do to other people.

It is not certain that all these oracles were spoken at the same time. But whoever collected the words of Amos has arranged them to lead up to a final speech of condemnation. This litany of horrors reaches a shocking and unexpected climax. The last condemnation is directed against the kingdom of Israel itself.

The sins of the people are listed (2.6-16). They oppress the poor and the weak. With creative perversity, through bribery, through excessive interest and harsh repayment terms for debts, they buy and sell the lives of the poor. They are involved in the worship of pagan gods, even to the extent of participating in ritual prostitution at the shrines of these gods.

And all this is happening even though Yahweh brought the people of Israel out of slavery in Egypt, led them through the wilderness, protected them as they settled in the promised land. Israel's ingratitude in the face of Yahweh's love is the grossest insult of all. And when Yahweh tried to bring the people back to their senses by sending prophets to speak in his name, the arrogant response was to tell the prophets to be silent. Because of this, there is nothing left for Israel but disaster and destruction.

THE RICH OPPRESS THE POOR

Please read: 3.9–4.3; 8.4-10

As Amos came from his wandering up and down the lonely and desolate regions that served as pasture land for his flocks, he was appalled by what he saw in the cities of the northern kingdom. The rich owned both winter homes and villas in the higher, more open quarters where they might enjoy cooling breezes in the summer. The poor were packed into crowded slums with narrow streets. The rich designed expensively decorated living quarters. Furniture was inlaid with ivory. The poor had to make do with bare necessities. The wealthy women, whom Amos angrily calls "cows of Bashan" after an area noted for its fertile grazing land and sleek cattle, lounge and order drinks while planning new ways to extort from the poor.

What is wrong is not the economic reality, that there are rich and poor. What is wrong is that the wealthy do not care about their poor brothers and sisters whom Yahweh has also called into covenant with himself. What is wrong is that the wealthy do not hesitate to take advantage of the poor to increase their own wealth.

Amos invites neighboring peoples (Ashdod, Egypt) to witness the evils taking place on the mountain of Samaria, the capital city of Israel, the northern kingdom. Even these foreigners who have not experienced the love of Yahweh as Israel had will recognize the flagrant injustice at work among Yahweh's people.

The people are bringing God's punishment on themselves. An invading army will sweep through the land and destroy the pretentious homes. The elaborate decorations will be reduced to pathetic rubble. The scheming, self-indulgent women will be a gruesome sight as they are dragged away, living or dead, with hooks.

In 8.4-10, this theme is played again. The business people can hardly wait for the religious festivals, the new moon and the sabbath, to be over so that they can get back to money-making. They plot how to cheat in weighing out the grain they sell so that their profits will be even greater. They scheme to control the lives and freedom of the poor in whatever way will add to their own fortunes. But even if the rich have forgotten Yahweh, Yahweh has not forgotten the oppressed poor.

We meet here the expectation for a "day" in which Yahweh's justice will be clear to all. That day will mark the triumph of the order intended by Yahweh. The oppression and evil that seem to thrive will be wiped out. That day will be so frightening for those who deserve the wrath of Yahweh that it can be described in terms of the reaction of the people to the sun setting at midday, to darkness covering the earth in daytime. All the celebrations will be turned into mourning and all the songs into funeral hymns.

THE ABUSE OF RELIGION

Please read: 5.18-27

This day, "the day of Yahweh," is something to which all the people look forward. They are firmly convinced that they are God's people. When Yahweh's rule prevails once for all, they will be receiving rich rewards. Or so they think think!

Amos speaks to this expectation. The people want the day of Yahweh's judgment to come. But they do not realize what they are asking. His judgment will be heaviest on them! They expect light and brightness and they will actually be awarded darkness and gloom. They are in the ironic position of a man who stops to catch his breath, congratulating himself for having escaped from a lion. But he turns around just in time to see a bear reaching to crush him. Or in the position of a man who has just arrived safely in his home after some dangerous incident. He feels secure behind his locked doors but as he stretches out his hand against the wall to rest a moment, he is bitten by a snake. Just so unexpected will be the day of Yahweh, Yahweh's judgment, for those who have been deceiving themselves about their standing in relation to God.

The most repugnant self-deception was in religious practice. All the usual rituals honoring Yahweh: the feasts; the sacrifices; the processions with song, music, dance, were going on as usual. But there was no inner turning to Yahweh, no realization that to truly honor him, one must also care about one's brother and sister.

Amos thunders that Yahweh cares not at all for ceremony that carries with it nothing of the heart. He wants no more feasts, no more sacrifices, no more music and singing.

Amos is not condemning religious ritual as such. Ritual was too much a part of the tradition of Israel. The feelings of people toward God must be expressed in some outward way.

What Amos does condemn is hypocrisy. The processions, the prayers, the festivals, the sacrifices, the holy places, all proclaim that Yahweh is important to the lives of the people. But the way they live, taking advantage of the poor, shows that faith in Yahweh and the kind of God he is is not important to them at all.

The worship of Yahweh will be real if the people "let justice surge like water, and goodness like an unfailing stream."

"Justice" is the outcome of the proper functioning of a court. The court, when it works as it should, finds the innocent person in the right, the guilty in the wrong. In doing this, the court often acts as defender of the innocent person who is poor or without influence.

The word used for "goodness" means the proper living out of what relationships call for. Each Israelite stood in a special relationship of integrity, concern, brotherhood, to each other Israelite. This relationship was founded in the special relationship that all had with Yahweh, or rather that Yahweh had with them.

Israel's sin lies in the fact that the courts betrayed true judgment. Judges and witness were bribed to render judgment or testimony in favor of the rich against the poor. The proper relationship of Israelite to Israelite was pushed aside in favor of self-seeking. Israel is bringing upon itself the heavy hand of punishment.

AMOS' CALL TO REPENTANCE

Please read: 4.6-12

In the light of this sinfulness, Amos calls the people to return to Yahweh.

First he sarcastically invites the people to come to the sanctuaries, Bethel and Gilgal, and to carry out the ritual and sacrifices of which they are so fond. The invitation reflects the true worth of their offerings.

"Come to Bethel and sin,
to Gilgal, and sin the more."

All the religious activity is accompanied by the same tired chronicle of sinfulness.

Over the years, Yahweh had tried to call the people to repentance by taking away some of the things on which they were so dependent. He tried to make them realize through experience that beyond them and all that for which they were working, lying and cheating was Yahweh.

They had felt famine (v. 6), drought (vv. 7-8), destruction of crops (v. 9), defeat in war and plague (v. 10), some unnamed disaster equivalent to the destruction of Sodom and Gomorrah, possibly earthquake (v. 11).

Each of these experiences was part of an on-going plan of Yahweh to remind the people of their infidelity to him and the covenant they had with him and with each other. In Yahweh burned the desire that the people acknowledge their evil ways and turn again to him and to their responsibilities to one another. But the tragic refrain is repeated after each example of disaster. "Yet you returned not to me, says the LORD."

This is a constant refrain in the prophets. The prophetic invitation is to return to Yahweh, to the acceptance of his love and will. This is the call to conversion. But since the call to conversion has been rejected, there remains a final fate for Israel. "Prepare to meet your God, O Israel."

Self-seeking, cheating, irresponsible, hypocritical people will indeed meet the good, the true God. They have been making pilgrimages to the shrines to meet him in ceremonies there. The quality of their lives proves that this meeting has been false and empty. Now they will meet God in another way, a painful way. In his judgment.

HOPE FOR THE FUTURE

Please read: 9.7-15

Because the tone seems very different from the rest of Amos, scholars discuss whether or not these could be the words of Amos. Whatever the correct answer, we shall read this passage which ends the book of Amos on a note of hope.

In v. 7, Amos makes a very radical statement to Israel. By reason of its own virtues or qualities, it is no different to Yahweh than the Ethiopians, whom the Israelites considered an enslaved people. And the migration of Israel from Egypt was no different to Yahweh than the migration of their ancient enemies, the Philistines, from the island of Crete (Caphtor), or of the Arameans, the people to the north. In other words, the Israelites were Yahweh's special people, not because they earned that distinction through their integrity or talents, but simply because Yahweh, in his own goodness and wisdom, chose them. Because this people responded without generosity or sincerity, they would be destroyed.

Yet, the destruction would not be total. The evil would be wiped out but the life of God's people would continue. One day, Yahweh will bring about such a situation of goodness and prosperity that, in the lively images of Amos, there will not be enough time for the ordinary cycle of growth. The grain will grow so fast that the one who is harvesting will catch up with the one planting seed. The very mountains will run with the juice of the grape vines.

Some day, God's restored people will settle in their land, this time to remain forever.

THE MESSAGE OF AMOS

Amos' language, rugged and strong, reveals his background. Through that language, and in the face of what he encountered, Amos presented what he understood to be Yahweh's message to his people. For the relatively short time during which he prophesied, Amos' understanding of what the religion of Yahweh was all about crashed head on into what he saw in the cities and religious centers of Israel. To Amos, it was clear that there was a great gap between what being Yahweh's people meant and what those who were called to be Yahweh's people actually were.

Yahweh's view of righteousness differed from the view of the powerful in Israel. Riches were considered a sign of Yahweh's blessing, a sign of being right with God. Amos proclaimed that the rich were sinners and oppressors. Those who were truly right with God were the poor and afflicted who had to suffer the oppression of their wealthy neighbors.

Yahweh's judgment, the "day of Yahweh," was something that all Israelites looked forward to. This would be a time of vindication, a time when the good and the just would be marked as such by Yahweh. But Amos warned that what so many people eagerly expected would prove to be a disaster for them. The greedy and self-seeking would discover that the day of Yahweh would show them up for what they were, persons interested only in themselves with no real concern for Yahweh and their brothers and sisters.

Yahweh had entered into a covenant with his people. "I will be your God and you will be my people." So many thought that they were fulfilling their side of the relationship with Yahweh by going through the prescribed ceremonies at the various shrines. Amos challenged this complacency with the charge of hypocrisy. Real religion is tested and proved true by its effect on daily life. Ritual is empty and meaningless unless it is related to the way one lives.

Little else is known about Amos. Did the confrontation with the priest, Amaziah, at Bethel (7.10-17), end his proclamation? Did he live much longer? Did he return to his life of obscurity as a shepherd? These questions cannot be answered.

Amos is remembered not for the details of his life but for the truth of his message spoken in the name of Yahweh. And that is the way he would have wanted it.

SUGGESTIONS FOR REFLECTION

1. How did the meaning of "prophet" differ in the days of Amos from the way we use it today? How was it similar to our contemporary meaning?

2. Amos was possibly a rough, country-type, poor and a bit crude in dress and the ways of civilized, cultured society, and he was not a prophet by profession, so he was rejected by the priest at the sanctuary of Bethel. He did not meet the expectations of someone speaking in Yahweh's name. Would he and his message have been better received if he had appeared otherwise? What would make a prophet and his message acceptable today?

3. How do the concerns of Yahweh in the prophesies of Amos foreshadow the later understanding that he is God of all peoples, not only his chosen ones, the Israelites?

4. Which abominations in this book defied the first three commandments? Which ones violated the other commandments? Why is Yahweh especially angry at these latter? Are any of these historical sins being committed today? If so, where and how?

5. What are a few key indications in the book of Amos that Yahweh definitely favors the poor? How does the condition of being poor make a man's relationship to Yahweh more honest? Which condition, poverty or riches, has seemed to you to be a sign of God's favor?

6. How were even the practices of religion seen to be evil? Is a similar self-deception still observable in some practice of religion today?

7. How could all the evils condemned by Amos be ultimately rooted in improper relationships between God and man, and person to person?

8. "To Amos it was clear that there was a great gap between what being Yahweh's people meant and what those who were called to be Yahweh's people actually were." How do we know that this same gap continued into the time of Jesus? Has it been closed yet among the people of God? In you?

9. The Israelites had looked forward to the "day of Yahweh" or the day of judgment to be a time of reward. Amos warned that it might be just the opposite, a time of vindication. Do lives of people today seem to be lived in expectation of such a day? If so, which type of "day" do they usually anticipate? What would Amos say to us today about this if he were to appear now at our national shrine?

10. In Chapter 1 Amos describes abominable sins of the pagans and quotes the Lord seven times, "Thus says the Lord: For three crimes of . . . and for four, I will not revoke my word . . . " Pretend He is speaking to us today in the 20th century, and write His description to finish that prophesy as He might to us, "Because they . . . ."

CHAPTER III

HOSEA AND THE LOVE OF GOD

HOSEA, HIS TIMES

The historical situation from which Hosea emerges and to which he speaks is the same as that of Amos. Hosea's prophetic activity begins about the year 750 B.C. Like Amos, Hosea directs his words to the kings and people of the northern kingdom. Like Amos, he is appalled by the empty religious practice, the infidelity to Yahweh, the injustices inflicted by the people of Israel on the weak and poor among them.

Unlike Amos, whose prophetic career was brief, Hosea spoke to events in the life of Israel through a period of at least ten, perhaps many more, years. The end of that period was a tragic one for Israel, marked as it was by the capture of Israel by the armies of Assyria in 721.

Even before this drastic climax, Hosea's preaching reflects hard days in Israel. Israel had participated in a rebellion against Assyria. In 733, the Assyrian king, Tiglath-Pileser, led an army into Israel, devastated the land, deported a large part of the population and took over much of the territory of Israel, leaving only the city of Samaria and a small area as a fragile fragment of the once proud kingdom.

HOSEA HIMSELF

We learn little about the details of Hosea's life from reading his words. His preaching took place mostly in the capital city of Samaria and at the sacred places of Gilgal and Bethel. He probably addressed crowds of people gathered at the sanctuaries and in the public places in the city. One event in his life does stand out and give his prophecy a special quality. This event was his marriage.

HOSEA'S MARRIAGE

Please read: 1.2–3.5

An experience that seared the heart of Hosea was the infidelity of his wife, Gomer. Even though she left him, Hosea could not restrain the deep passion that burned within him. He loved Gomer and wanted desperately to have her back.

Many men and women through history have experienced the pain of an unfaithful spouse. And they have found that rejection by their partner could not destroy the love they felt.

What is remarkable about Hosea is that he relates this experience to the intensity of Yahweh's love for his people. Yahweh is like a husband who has been deserted by his unfaithful wife, Israel. Yet his love never ceases. He continues to love and to call his spouse back to him.

The language of prostitution permeates much of the preaching of Hosea. The girl he marries will both be a prostitute and represent the harlotry of the people. The sexual language and imagery is very much to the point. The people prostitute themselves in the worship of the god, Baal.

Baal was a god of the Canaanite religion. According to the popular belief, he brought the rain in the late autumn and winter. This rain was absolutely essential if crops were to grow.

The earth was envisioned as a goddess impregnated by the rain from the god. The ritual celebrated in honor of the god included an acted-out suggestion or encouragement for him to have intercourse with the earth. Men had intercourse with prostitutes associated with the sanctuaries. Other women aside from the professional prostitutes also presented themselves to male worshippers for the sexual activity that would insure the fertility of the land.

"Harlotry" is an apt name for Israel's behavior because it has abandoned its true husband, Yahweh, and is pursuing a false lover, Baal. And the language of sexual promiscuity is very appropriate because the ceremonies in honor of this god involve ritual sex.

It is not certain whether Gomer's prostitution was of this religious nature alone or whether her activities were on a broader scale. In either case, prostitute she is.

In the course of their marriage, Hosea's wife bears three children. These children are given names which signify Yahweh's message. The very presence of the children will be living evidence of his attitude toward his people.

The first son is named "Jezreel." Jezreel was the name of a plain in Israel and of a town on that plain. About one hundred years before Hosea began to prophesy, a man named Jehu had carried out a coup against the king of Israel and assassinated him. He had ordered the execution of the royal family and had their heads sent to him at Jezreel.

Hosea's son, Jezreel, is to be testimony to the fact that Yahweh will punish the family of Jehu, still reigning in Israel, and destroy the kingdom itself.

The second child born to Hosea and Gomer was a daughter named "Lo-ruhama," literally, "she has found no pity," or "unpitied." Her name testifies that Yahweh no longer feels tenderness and care for his people. The very mention of her name in public would be something of a scandal. It would convey an unnatural situation—a father without love for his baby daughter. But Yahweh is justified in his feeling toward his people because they have been unfaithful to their covenant with him.

The third child, a son, Hosea calls "Lo-ammi," "Not-my-people." The formula expressing the relationship between Yahweh and his people has been, "You will be my people and I will be your God." Yahweh's very name conveys that he is the One who is always present to his people. He is the One who saves, who liberates. He is involved in their lives and in what happens to them. But they have ceased to be his people. They have lusted after the gods of Canaan. Yahweh will therefore no longer be savior and deliverer to them. The only possible outcome is tragedy.

2.4-15 vividly presents Yahweh's charge. Yahweh is the wronged, rejected husband who brings suit against his faithless wife. Israel has pursued the worship of the god, Baal, because it believed that this god controlled nature. Baal gave the land fertility to bring forth wheat and grapes and lush pasturage. Israel is a self-seeking prostitute running after her lovers (Baal) for the pay that will be thrown to her. They "give me my bread and my water, my wool and my flax, my oil and my drink."

Israel will learn the hard way that Yahweh is the God who has provided the bounties of nature for Israel. Yahweh will end Israel's self-deception by taking away the fruits of the earth. Baal will stand exposed as the powerless nothing that he is.

This will be only the first step in Yahweh's design for his fickle people. Beginning with 2.16, he reveals his intentions.

Hosea speaks of the time of the wandering in the desert as an ideal period. There, cut off from Egypt, surrounded by barrens offering little food or water, the people had to depend totally on Yahweh. When they settled in the land, became a powerful people, enjoyed the fruits of their labors, they forgot that dependence and began to rely on themselves and the gods of the land.

Yahweh will lead his people once again to a situation in which their former love for one another can be renewed. In that new situation, Israel would realize that only Yahweh is God. When Yahweh and his people are reconciled, everything around them will be at peace; the "beasts of the field," "the birds of the air," "the things that crawl on the ground."

The new love between Yahweh and his people will be all that it should be and will last forever. This joyousness will be mirrored in the bounteous fertility of the soil.

In vv. 24-5, the names which Hosea had given to his children as a commentary on Israel's situation once more come into play. The name "Jezreel" was a warning that the crimes committed there would be punished. Now it reverts to its original meaning, "God will sow." God will sow the land and guarantee its fruitfulness. Yahweh will again feel tenderness and compassion for "Lo-ruhama," "Unpitied." And the people whose infidelity earned for them the designation, "Lo-ammi," "Not my people,"

Yahweh will once again call "My people." They in turn will respond with the shout of fidelity to the covenant, "My God."

In 3.1-5, Hosea's own life reflects Yahweh's attitudes. It is difficult to know how this passage relates to chapter 1, whether it is another account of the situation related there, or whether it is a subsequent development. Whatever the case may be, it tells that Hosea and Gomer had some kind of preliminary reconciliation. However, the wife whom he loved he did not take to himself immediately. There was to be a time of testing before they took up their lives together. This represented what must happen to Israel before it could truly open itself to Yahweh's embrace. It would lose its rulers ("without king and prince"), its religious institutions ("without sacrifice or sacred pillar, without ephod or household idols"). Then would Israel recognize and rush to its only support and God.

Here we meet the call to "turn back" or "return" to Yahweh. This is the familiar language of conversion in the prophets. Their goal is to have the people turn away from the crooked, treacherous and deceptive path on which they are walking and return to Yahweh, their only true peace and happiness.

This lengthy passage sums up the tremendous insight Hosea has into Yahweh's love. In daring language, Hosea expresses Yahweh's feelings as burning with all the passion of a loving but betrayed husband. His rejected love will bring punishment and disaster, but even that leads to the rebirth of love that lasts forever.

One thing should be clear at this stage. Any attempt to put into simple prose the fiery preaching of the prophets produces something very tame by comparison. The brief explanations are important for understanding the prophetic message. But it is even more important to read the words of the prophets and to hear them as the impassioned outcries of God-driven men desperately trying to call their people back to the truth and life of God.

YAHWEH'S CONSTANT LOVE

Please read: 11.1-11

What makes the infidelity of Israel so terrible is that it is the sadly out-of-place response to the great love of Yahweh.

At the beginning of Israel's life, Yahweh freed it from slavery in Egypt. Yahweh was, and is, like a tenderhearted father who takes a child in his arms, who presses it to his cheeks, who supports the toddler as it takes its first shaky steps. And Israel has been like a petulant child who reaches not for the person offering love, but for some stranger offering shiny, but cheap, toys.

The stranger offering the cheap toys is Egypt. Egypt, encouraging illusory dreams of freedom, has been inciting Israel to revolt against Assyria. Israel had been taught to trust in Yahweh alone and not rely on political power plays. Now Israel has become like any other rebellious nation and it will be punished by Assyria for its rebellion. The stubborn son of Yahweh richly deserves this disaster. But then Yahweh's breaking heart speaks again. "How can I give you up, O Israel?"

Can Yahweh let his disobedient people be treated like the cities of Admah and Zeboiim which, in the old story, were burned to ashes with Sodom and Gomorrah? No! Yahweh is "God and not man, the Holy One present among you." His purpose, his way of acting is his own. No matter what happens, his love endures.

From Egypt, to which many Israelites fled as refugees from the wrath of Assyria, and from Assyria to which many were deported, Israel shall one day return to settle once again in its own land.

In this magnificent section, the love of Yahweh for his people is seen from yet another perspective. The love of husband and wife portrayed in the first three chapters, as deep as it may be, is not enough to express all the riches of the divine love. Yahweh's love is also the tender love of a father for his helpless child. When this love is rejected, the father, like the husband, continues to love despite ingratitude.

THE CRIME OF ISRAEL

Please read: 4.1-3

Yahweh charges the people with their sins. There is no "fidelity" or "mercy," i.e., integrity in their relationships with God and one another. And there is no "knowledge of Yahweh," a favorite expression of Hosea. The people do not "know," that is to say, appreciate and live out the implications of the fact that Yahweh is the source of their life, their freedom, their good.

Instead, the land is filled with all kinds of injustice and sinfulness. Because of this, the whole land is polluted and will be flooded with the results of this sinfulness.

THE CRIME OF THE PRIESTS

Please read: 4.4-10

The priests were supposed to preserve and teach the real knowledge of Yahweh. But they had failed miserably in this privilege and responsibility.

And so, probably while standing in one of the great shrines of Israel, Hosea indicts the priests assembled there. Crowds have come to hear the teaching of the priests. Instead, they hear Hosea's stinging accusations.

The priests were to help the people understand what the covenant and commandments meant as the circumstances of life changed. These priests have allowed the religion of Yahweh to become riddled with the superstitions and immorality of the paganism around them. They have neglected to challenge the people to recognize their obligations to one another. They have made their priestly position simply the means to foster their own welfare. They have watered down dynamic faith in Yahweh to a mixture of magic and self-serving.

For this, their already corrupted priesthood will be taken away from them and their families. All their rituals are sterile, their religious activities barren, because the religion they propose is nothing more than prostitution, infidelity to the real relationship between Yahweh and his people.

THE CRIME OF THE LEADERS

Please read: 5.1-2

The king and his court were meant to be servants of Yahweh, instruments of his justice and right. But they too have followed their own way, using their position for their own purposes. They too, probably at some festive gathering at which all the royal celebrities were present, feel the bite of Hosea's words.

The leaders of Israel are expected to render true justice and to have it applied to themselves. Instead, they have trapped the people in a tangle of bribery, corruption, perjury, deceit. Using images from hunting, Hosea describes their activities as being like the snare that snaps closed on unwary birds or the hidden net which entraps the unsuspecting animal. These crimes are connected with certain places; Mizpah, Tabor. Why this connection is made is no longer clear. What is clear is that kings and officials have been derelict in their duties to lead, to direct the people in the ways of Yahweh and to protect the rights of all, especially the poor, as God's people.

INSINCERE CONVERSION

Please read: 5.8–6.7

The prophets were men of their times. They spoke to their world, to the political, moral and religious situations around them. The names and references that are mysterious to us were household words to the prophets and their contemporaries.

Here, Hosea is addressing a very real and significant event in the life of his people.

Political intrigue was taken as a matter of course. As might be expected, the intrigue focused on the realities of power. Egypt and Mesopotamia were the political giants. Palestine was a narrow connecting link between them. Naturally, there was constant rivalry between the great powers to extend their influence into the land that both separated and joined them.

Sometimes Egypt dominated; sometimes a country of Mesopotamia did. If one became much stronger than the other, it would simply push its way into Israel and Judah. If neither had the upper hand, they balanced one another and the lands between them were able to shape their own destinies with relatively little interference. At this particular time, Assyria in Mesopotamia was riding high, recognized as the force to be reckoned with. Egypt was like the cowardly lion, not up to full-scale war with Assyria but encouraging the lands subject to Assyria to rebel.

The little kingdoms of Palestine, Israel among them, are organizing a united revolt against Assyria. They want the southern kingdom of Judah in their ranks. When the king of Judah refuses to join the conspiracy, the rebellious coalition invades Judah, planning to put a king more co-operative with their plans on the throne. When the invasion begins, the desperate king of Judah calls on the king of Assyria for help. The Assyrian king responds with force. The fierce Assyrian army puts down the rebellion. Its king takes control of most of the kingdom of Israel and sends a large part of the population into exile.

Hosea speaks to this situation about 733 B.C. In v. 8, the prophet is commanded to be like the city lookout who must blow the trumpet to warn the people of an advancing army. The enemy forces move from the south from town to town; Gibeah, Ramah, Bethel. The territory of Ephraim, one of the tribes of the northern kingdom whose name is used to represent all Israel, will be laid waste.

There is even danger from the southern kingdom of Judah. Now that the Assyrian army has battered the northern kingdom, Judah takes advantage of this weakness to move into the territory of Israel on its northern boundary (v. 10).

Why has all this happened? Because instead of remaining faithful to Yahweh, both Israel and Judah have preferred to play power politics. They have appealed to foreigners for help. To accept foreign domination meant to accept foreign meddling in religion and national life. To accept foreign domination revealed a lack of trust in Yahweh.

But the passing power of Assyria is not the answer to anything. In brutally realistic language, Hosea describes the might of Yahweh as a moth and maggots already working within the diseased kingdoms of Israel and Judah, and as a lion that not even Assyria can drive off.

In v. 15, Yahweh asserts that he will withdraw his help and assistance. The reason for this is not petty vengeance or anger. Rather, the people, now powerless, will again come to recognize their total dependence on Yahweh.

There were public ceremonies of penance or conversion, just as we have penance services today. In 6.1-3, Hosea repeats the words of the ritual. The people say, "Come, let us return to the LORD." The people acknowledge, or so they say, that they have brought the punishment of Yahweh on themselves. If they return to him, in a short time, "after two days, on the third day," he will restore them to their previous prosperity. If they "know" Yahweh again–and the people believe that this happens through their ritual–Yahweh will make his power felt among them. His restored presence will be like the spring rain that brings the dry earth to life.

But Yahweh complains that the conversion of the people is a passing thing (vv. 4-5). It is like dew on the grass in the early morning. This dries up as soon as the heat of the sun touches it. This fickle lack of fidelity has been the reason for the tribulations that have fallen upon the people.

What Yahweh wants is not empty ceremonies but true and sincere conversion. True religion involves the sincere commitment to Yahweh, to the kind of living God that he is, to the vital relationship he has with his people, to the concerns that all those who are Yahweh's people ought to have for each other.

THE CALL TO REPENTANCE

Please read: 14.2-9

The book of Hosea ends with a call to what Hosea always hoped for and what Yahweh wished, Israel's recognition of the error of its ways and its return to Yahweh in tenderness and love. Hosea encourages the people to true repentance. When Israel lives a good life, then it can render honestly and with integrity its sacrificial ritual, "the offerings of bullocks."

True repentance will recognize that the power of Assyria or of armed calvary will not save it. True repentance will see the emptiness of the idols fashioned by human craftsmen.

Vv. 5-9 indicate Yahweh's response to true conversion on Israel's part. Despite the past, Yahweh loves his people tenderly and deeply. He will be for his people like the early morning dew which, in the hot and dry Near East, is so important for making things grow.

Israel will again be beautiful and luxuriant like an olive tree, like the magnificent fragrant cedars that grow on Mt. Lebanon. The people will live in the shelter of Yahweh and be known to all as good and beautiful. And all this happens simply because of Yahweh's love. "Because of me you bear fruit!"

THE MESSAGE OF HOSEA

Eight pages of printed word do not seem to be much output for thirty years of comment on the life of Israel. That is all there is from Hosea in our Bibles.

However, those eight pages capture an intensity of personal experience for Hosea, an intimacy with Yahweh, an ability to read with blazing clarity the decadence of Israel's religious, political and social life.

Hosea is a powerful antidote for those who would see Yahweh of the Hebrew Scriptures as a God of wrath only. For Hosea, Yahweh loves like a new husband, like a new father. The passion of his love is such that it outlasts infidelity and rejection by the beloved.

The infidelity of the people showed itself in manifold ways. There was the desire to share in the sexually oriented nature religion of the land in which Israel had settled. There was the indiscriminate mixing of elements from this religion with the religion of Yahweh. There was the lack of leadership from priests and kings: those who were to direct in the way of Yahweh followed the attractive paths that led to more wealth, more power for themselves. There was the corruption of justice and right order being deftly executed by the upper classes to enrich themselves at the expense of the poor and helpless. There was the attempt to further national interests by a system of alliances with countries around them. Basic to all these was a lack of trust in Yahweh.

The meaning of life in Israel was no longer seen as service of Yahweh and neighbor. Yahweh was no longer accepted as the one who gave direction and meaning to life. The people found a better way to get what they thought was important. And the way of Yahweh had little to do with that. Their decadence and manipulations deserved disaster. There was no escape from that.

But Yahweh's love brought good even from the inevitable disaster. Israel would turn to Yahweh again. Their new union would be lasting, joyful, the source of peace for the whole world.

SUGGESTIONS FOR REFLECTION

1. In contrast to Amos' litanies of sins of which the Israelites were guilty, Hosea focuses in on the sin of idolatry, which he sees as infidelity, unfaithfulness to the

God of the covenant. Describe how his inspiration came from his own life experience.

2. When his people were helpless in the desert, and had to depend totally on Yahweh, they were faithful to him. When his gifts brought affluence, and self-reliance took over, the people became unfaithful. Recall a time in your life when helplessness kept you faithful to God, or perhaps, a time when you forgot your dependence upon him, and strayed into infidelity towards him. Reflect on and describe your feelings through either experience.

3. Write three words that might describe the attitude of Yahweh towards his people in the book of Hosea.

4. Which, in your opinion, is a more powerful example of the abiding love of Yahweh for his people, the loving, forgiving husband of an unfaithful wife, or the tenderly loving father for a helpless child? Which speaks more personally to you?

5. Hosea calls attention to the sins of the leaders in Israel—the priests and kings. What were their sins as he detailed them? Were his words received gratefully?

6. When Israel and Judah begin to put their confidence in the strength of a political ally, Assyria, rather than in Yahweh alone, they are misplacing their trust. How did this attitude begin? Why was it so strong?

7. If Yahweh's treatment of Israel's infidelity was not revenge or anger, then why did he punish his people?

8. How does Hosea's chapter 14 resemble Amos' chapter 9?

CHAPTER IV

WHAT IS A PROPHET? MORE

The first chapter of this book probed the phenomenon of prophecy and recalled early prophets about whom we read in the Hebrew Scriptures.

With Amos and Hosea, we face a new situation. For these prophets and others who came after them, we have collections of their sayings. This was not the case with the earlier prophets. Because we know at least some of what they prophesied, we are able to add a great deal to our understanding of what being a prophet meant.

THE HEART OF PROPHECY

Fundamental to prophecy is the conviction in the prophet that he or she has shared in the world of the divine and is being pressed by a divine power to communicate to others what has been learned from the experience. Amos and Hosea share that conviction. They repeat expressions like, "The LORD said to me," "Thus says the LORD," "This is what the LORD God showed me."

Amos and Hosea must share what they know. "Hear the word of the LORD, O people of Israel." "Hear this word, O men of Israel, that the LORD pronounces over you." "Hear and bear witness against the house of Jacob, says the Lord GOD, the God of hosts."

The words of Amos and Hosea are the fiery proclamations of God-driven men. The occasion for delivery may have been an assembly for some religious celebration at one of the shrines of Israel. It may have been some festival in the cities where kings and nobles sat watching holiday processions.

While the priests went through the sacrificial rituals, Amos and Hosea cried out that the ritual was hypocrisy. While the official prophets attached to the royal court told the king that all was well, Amos and Hosea stripped away the attractive covering that masked the decay eating away at the life of God's people.

WORKING UP TO PROPHECY

For some prophets met in the first chapter, ecstasy was a relatively common occurrence. The prophet spoke his piece while in some abnormal state.

This is not the case with Amos and Hosea and the rest of the classical prophets generally. There is no indication that being "out of their minds" was common for them. In fact, the evidence points in the opposite direction. They were very much rational men when they spoke.

Where did their prophetic message come from? What gave them the conviction that they were speaking for Yahweh? Amos and Hosea and the other prophets we will read from now on often speak as if they have heard the actual, physical words of Yahweh.

In the following passages Amos describes himself in conversation with Yahweh.

"This is what the Lord GOD showed me: a basket of ripe fruit. 'What do you see, Amos?' he asked. I answered, 'A basket of ripe fruit.' Then the LORD said to me:

The time is ripe to have done with my people Israel;
I will forgive them no longer." (8.1-2).

"This is what the LORD God showed me: He was forming a locust swarm when the late growth began to come up . . . While they were eating all the grass in the land, I said:

Forgive, O Lord GOD!
How can Jacob stand?
He is so small!

And the LORD repented of this. 'It shall not be,' said the Lord GOD." (7.1-3)

How are we to understand expressions like these? Did the prophet close himself in his room and actually hear the voice of God and his words thundering around him? Did the prophet have extraordinary visions as a matter of course?

The answer to these questions would seem to be, "No." That the prophet was convinced that he was communicating the word of Yahweh did not depend on extraordinary sights and sounds.

The prophet knew and lived with every fiber of his being what having Yahweh as his God meant. He knew the traditions of Israel, especially the tradition that Yahweh had liberated the people from slavery. He believed in the covenant relationship that was supposed to exist between Yahweh and his people and among the people themselves. He appreciated the kind of fidelity that Yahweh deserved and the kind of mutual concern that ought to characterize any people that was truly Yahweh's people. He recognized evil and corruption around him.

Amos, as he walked the streets of Samaria, the capital of Israel, could see for himself the great gap between the rich and the poor. No doubt he heard the poor complain about how they were being victimized by high rates of interest on the money they borrowed and by corrupt judges who could be bribed to favor the rich. Amos could observe the poverty-stricken farmer bent in backbreaking labor while the wealthy manipulator of goods and money lounged in his villa. Amos could join the processions to the sacred shrines where religious ceremonies were carried out with pomp and splendor. The blatant hypocrisy gnawed at him.

Amos could also keep up with what was going on on the international scene. He knew as well as anyone else at the time the never-ending power struggle between the great states. He heard the rumors about the fierce giant to the north, Assyria, and its insatiable appetite for conquest. He could foresee, as could any other astute observer, that Israel was part of the conquest schedule. Hadn't it always happened that way?

But there was one element more, a crucial one. Amos was convinced that his belief in Yahweh was not only something that had been bred into him. It was alive and real. Right now Yahweh was touching his life. Yahweh's spirit was providing his insights, guaranteeing their truth and moving him irresistably to voice them.

His anger and disgust at the treatment of Israelite by Israelite, at the empty rituals performed at the shrines, was not simply the wrath of a social reformer. It was the truth that Yahweh wanted him to communicate.

The political and military turbulence around him was not simply the result of power against power and intrigue against intrigue. The destruction that would come had more meaning than that. It was Israel's punishment for infidelity to Yahweh, the source of life and good.

In other words, Amos and the other classical prophets are not prophets because of mystical experiences. They are men of their religion, men of their times, men of their own personal background.

But also common to them all is the burning conviction that what they say is not of their own making. However they arrived at their insights into the present and the future, Yahweh was responsible for the process. And that they speak is not their own doing. Yahweh drives them to speak.

Amos says it clearly. The priest at the holy place at Bethel commanded Amos to stop preaching because he was disturbing the people and the king. Amos answered, "I was a shepherd . . . The LORD took me from following the flock, and said to me, Go, prophesy to my people Israel." (7.14-15) Amos was not his own man. He was Yahweh's man.

HOW THE PROPHET UNDERSTOOD HIMSELF: THE COVENANT

Volume II of this series explains an idea which is fundamental to understanding the religion of Israel. That notion is covenant. The basic historical experience that formed the religion of Israel was the Exodus. Yahweh had freely chosen to intervene in the life of a group of slaves and liberate them from bondage in Egypt. More than an act of sympathy or compassion, Yahweh's act was part of a plan for the total liberation of all creation. How this was to happen was not clear, nor was this vast vision always understood and appreciated. However, Israel did believe that its God saved and freed.

Israel tried to put into words the relationship between Yahweh and itself that Yahweh had freely chosen to establish. Influenced by the thought world of its time, Israel expressed this relationship in terms of the treaties between kings common on the contemporary political scene.

The relationship between Yahweh and Israel was like that between a great king who chose to enter into an agreement with a lesser king. The terms of the agreement called for mutual loyalty and assistance. Of course, it was not exactly the same between Yahweh and his people. The people could not help Yahweh. They could not make demands on him because of some treaty terms. What existed between Yahweh and his people was the spontaneous doing of Yahweh.

But there was a kind of exchange. Most simply put, the covenant was Yahweh saying, "I will be your God," and the people responding, "We will be your people."

For Yahweh to be God was not a static relationship, something inscribed on a document. Yahweh would always be to his people what he had been to the slaves in Egypt, one who freed, who saved from the dangers and threats to life.

On the other hand, the people would pledge themselves to be Yahweh's people. This included religious ritual and ceremonial but went far beyond that. It called for the kind of life that would reflect the goodness, the truth, the integrity of Yahweh. It demanded absolute fidelity to Yahweh and the refusal to follow other gods or things that pass for gods, like wealth, power, pleasure.

This notion of covenant or treaty by itself did not adequately express the richness of the relationship between Yahweh and his people. We have seen, for example, that Hosea saw the relationship between Yahweh and his people as the love between husband and wife, or that between father and child. Still, the notion of covenant remains central in the Scriptures and for the prophets.

HOW THE PROPHET UNDERSTOOD HIMSELF: THE MESSENGER OF YAHWEH ACCUSING THE PEOPLE OF INFIDELITY

Reflected in the sayings of the prophets is the understanding that they are messengers, spokesmen for Yahweh. They speak in his name to Israel and to other nations. Sometimes they bring comfort and hope with promises of good and peace to come. More often, they accuse Israel of infidelity and tell of the punishment that can be expected.

The prophets fit into the background of their times.

When a king violated a treaty, the offended king would send a messenger to protest and complain against the offender. The indictment the messenger voiced often recalled the past relationship between the kings and told how the offended king had shown kindness to his unfaithful vassal. The crimes or offenses were then detailed. The indictment ended either with a declaration of war as punishment for the infidelity or the issuing of an ultimatum demanding that the terms of the treaty be adhered to.

In much of the prophetic material, the prophets appear as messengers of Yahweh who is the injured party in a broken treaty situation. Israel is the violator of the covenant. The prophet is the spokesman who presents Yahweh's complaint. A clear example of this approach can be found in the book of the prophet Micah. He was roughly a contemporary of Amos and Hosea but directed his words to the southern kingdom of Judah.

Chapter 6 of Micah begins:

"Hear, then, what the LORD says:
Arise, present your plea before the mountains,
and let the hills hear your voice!
Hear, O mountains, the plea of the LORD,
pay attention, O foundations of the earth!
For the LORD has a plea against his people,
and he enters into trial with Israel."

The Hebrew word translated "plea" is *rib* (pronounced *reev*) which means "lawsuit," "legal dispute." Yahweh calls on the mountains and hills to be witnesses in the lawsuit that he has against his people.

Then comes the recollection of all that Yahweh has been and done for his people.

"O my people, what have I done to you,
or how have I wearied you? Answer me!
For I brought you up from the land of Egypt,
from the place of slavery I released you . . . "

The people respond to Yahweh's recalling of his love and favors by asking if he wishes them to perform religious rituals.

"With what shall I come before the LORD,
and bow before God most high?
Shall I come before him with holocausts,
with calves a year old?"

In a beautiful passage, Micah indicates the heart of true religion.

"You have been told, O man, what is good,
and what the LORD requires of you:
Only to do the right and to love goodness,
and to walk humbly with your God."

The word translated here as "goodness" is the Hebrew *hesed* which means fidelity to the covenant, to truly being Yahweh's people with all that means.

For Micah and the other prophets, all the aspects of daily life came under the influence of the covenant between Yahweh and his people. The prophets were charged with presenting Yahweh's indictment for the disregard and violation of the covenant. They confronted Israel squarely with the seriousness of its failings and with the terrible results to be expected from cutting itself away from the living God of Israel. The prophets offered Israel a chance to return to Yahweh, to "walk humbly with . . . God."

PROPHETIC CONFLICT

The prophets had problems. People do not want to hear that they are sinners, that they are hypocrites, that they have been lying and cheating. Very often, they resent being called to reform. We all like to think we have things figured out for ourselves. We do not enjoy moving out of a way of life into which we have settled comfortably.

Amos clashed with his hearers. When he criticized Israel at the very heart of its religious life, the sanctuary at Bethel, the priest in charge tried to silence him. Hosea tells us that the people said of him:

"The prophet is a fool
the man of the spirit is mad!" (9.7)

This hostility and rejection was the almost universal experience of the prophets.

The content of the prophetic message explains the hostility. Kings were charged with being untrustworthy and self-seeking. Priests were accused of dereliction of duty in not instructing the people in the ways of Yahweh. The professional prophets on the royal payroll and those who served on the staffs of the sanctuaries were condemned for speaking the soothing and approving words the kings and people wanted to hear rather than the pure call to follow Yahweh. The wealthy and powerful had to swallow being characterized as liars, hypocrites, oppressors of the poor. It is no wonder the prophets were not popular.

THE FORM OF THE PROPHETIC MESSAGE

The book of Hosea has fourteen chapters; the book of Amos, nine. It is important to remember that the book came after the prophecy. The prophets generally did not write. They spoke. Often, their messages were brief and in poetic form.

The chapter divisions and sub-headings in our modern Bibles do not necessarily represent actual individual prophecies. In fact, it is rather difficult to determine with certainty where each message began and ended, although there are sometimes indications.

For example, Hosea 4.1 begins, "Hear the word of the LORD, O people of Israel." But 4.4 is clearly addressed to a more limited group. "With you is my grievance, O priests!" Thus, 4.1-3 concerns all the people while 4.4-14 focuses on the priests and their faults. But even that is no proof that all of 4.4-14 was spoken at the same time. There seem to be divisions within it.

Again, 5.1 is addressed to three groups; the priests, all Israel, the royal court. But 5.8 contains the command to "blow the horn . . . the trumpet." Usually this kind of command is directed to the prophet who is put into the role of a watchman warning the people of approaching danger. Thus, 5.8 begins a new section. But this does not guarantee that 5.1-7 was all spoken at the same time. It might be a small collection of similar prophecies.

The point is that the prophet, in this case Hosea, did not speak a book. He spoke prophecies which were often brief, often in poetic form.

Since the prophetic messages were often brief, it was fairly easy for the followers or sympathizers of the prophet to remember them. These people memorized what the prophet had said and later someone wrote it down. Writers used their own techniques for organizing the sayings that were preserved. They might connect a series of oracles delivered against the priests, even if they were spoken at different times. They might bring together oracles that were related to a specific historical situation, e.g., a foreign invasion, even if these oracles had actually been spoken over a period of days or months.

In the course of time, these smaller collections were organized into a larger one, the book as we have it today.

The book of the prophet Micah has a very simple arrangement.

Chapters 1–3, threats of judgment; 4–5, hope and promise of salvation; 6.1–7.7, threats of judgment; 7.8–7.20, hope and promise of salvation.

THE FORM OF PROPHECY: HEBREW POETRY

Much of what the prophet said was poetry. Bibles indicate this by setting prose sections into lines of equal length while setting poetic sections in lines of unequal length.

Following this rule, the reader using the New American Bible can readily see that the book of Amos is mostly in poetry. Prose sections are 1.1; 3.1; 3.13; sections of chapter 7; 8.1-2 and 9.1. The rest is poetry.

Hebrew poetry is different from the poetry with which we are most familiar. It does not rhyme. It does not end lines with words that sound the same; June, moon; place, face; peeping, creeping. It does have a rhythm, a certain number of beats to each line, but this is difficult to bring out in translation.

There is one characteristic of Hebrew poetry which is obvious even in translation. It is called "parallelism." Each line of poetry is divided into two, three or four parts. Each of these parts is related in thought to the other or others. Amos 8.4-6 can serve as an example. The first part of the line is:
"Hear this, you who trample upon the needy."
The second part of the line picks up this thought and carries it further:
"and destroy the poor of the land!"
"Destroy the poor of the land" is another powerful way of repeating "trample on the needy."

The first part of v. 5 reads:
" 'When will the new moon be over,' you ask"
The second part of the line elaborates on this. Why do the people want the new moon, a religious festival, to be over?
"that we may sell our grain."
The next part of v. 5 has three sections. Each describes the kind of business the oppressors are planning.
" 'We will diminish the ephah' (a measure roughly equivalent to a bushel)
'add to the shekel' (a measure of weight)

'and fix our scales for cheating.' "
In other words, these business people plot to tamper with the measures and weights used in selling grain and other items of trade.

Characteristic of Hebrew poetry is that each of these short units in some way repeats or carries further the original idea.

The same is true in v. 6, which has three parts. The first describes the perverse plans of the wealthy.
" 'We will buy the lowly man for silver' "
The second expresses the same obsession with bribery and corruption in different words.
" '(we will buy) the poor man for a pair of sandals' "
The third part of the line moves this preoccupation into a different area.
" 'Even the refuse of the wheat we will sell!"

These examples illustrate that Hebrew poetry is rather free compared to most of the poetry with which we are probably familiar. It is not easy for us, reading English translations, to catch the beat of the rhythm. However, we can get to appreciate the connection of ideas within a line of poetry.

WHO IS A PROPHET: SUMMARY

This is a good place to sum up the chief points to remember about Amos, Hosea and the other prophets whom we call the classical prophets.

1. They are convinced that they speak for Yahweh to the people of their time.

2. They do not primarily foretell the future but challenge the people because of their faithlessness to Yahweh and one another.

3. They call the people to return to Yahweh and warn of disasters to come if true conversion does not take place.

4. They recall Yahweh's deep love and offer the hope that even the catastrophes that befall the people will bring about a return to Yahweh.

5. They often present themselves as messengers and their message as an indictment by Yahweh for the relationship broken by his people.

6. Usually, they did not write their messages but spoke them, often to the public. Their followers remembered and collected their sayings. Eventually these sayings were written down and collected in the form of our present "books." We do not necessarily have all the sayings of any prophet.

7. The prophets were often in conflict with the political and religious institutions of their time. They were opposed and rejected by those who were part of these institutions.

8. Much of what the prophets said is cast in the form of Hebrew poetry.

SUGGESTIONS FOR REFLECTION

1. "The classical prophets are not prophets because of mystical experiences. They are men of their religion, men of their times, men of their own personal background." Review how each, Hosea and Amos, was a man of religion, a man of his times, and a man of his own personal background.

2. "Yahweh's spirit was providing the prophet's insights, guaranteeing their truth and moving him irresistably to voice them . . . He was Yahweh's man." Is this the way you envisioned the inspiration of a prophet?

3. How does the idea of a prophet as one who pleads for the rights of Yahweh, a great king, in a covenant relationship with the nation, correspond with your concept of a prophet before taking this course?

4. Judging from the history of the classical prophets, would you expect a true prophet to be a popular and accepted person? What criteria could you use in evaluating a prophet's message? What problems can prophets as God's messengers usually anticipate?

5. What is the meaning of *hesed*? How is this word fundamental to each prophet's warning concerning the covenant relationship?

6. Explain how the prophetic words of Hosea and Amos came to be collected and recorded. What do we need to be conscious of when we are reading their messages?

7. Using the books of Micah, Amos, or Hosea, find several examples of Hebrew poetry that show parallelism or the repetition of an idea, or that carry further an original idea. What other characteristics of Hebrew poetry would help one to interpret these books?

8. Reflect on the words of Micah, chapter 6, verse 8. Why does this passage embody the heart of true religion?

CHAPTER V

ISAIAH AND THE HOLINESS OF GOD

The book of Isaiah in our Bibles has 66 chapters. However, careful reading reveals a sharp division at the end of chapter 39 and the beginning of chapter 40.

The historical situation changes. Chapters 1–39 speak to the people of Jerusalem and warn them about their sinfulness and the destruction that this sinfulness will bring upon them. Chapters 40–55 speak to people in exile, people who have already experienced the punishment threatened.

Chapters 1–39 are filled with admonitions and warnings. The mood of chapters 40–55 is consolation and hope. There are also differences in style and language. These and other considerations have given rise to widespread agreement today that the first 39 chapters of the book of Isaiah actually come from a man named Isaiah. The rest of the book is later, reflecting different times and different circumstances. There will be a later chapter on the unknown prophet responsible for chapters 40–55 and on his message.

ISAIAH, HIS TIMES

Isaiah emerges from the same historical setting as Hosea and Amos. His prophetic preaching spans 40 years, beginning about the year 740 B.C. He came on the scene just as a period of prosperity was coming to an end. His homeland, Judah, was to be involved in a series of crucial events in the ensuing years.

We have already seen how the dominant neighbor of Israel and Judah was Assyria to the north. As Egypt and Assyria struggled for power, Syria, Israel and Judah jockeyed for the position that would assure the greatest benefits, especially survival in independence.

Around 735 B.C., Syria and Israel became allies intent on rebellion against the domination of Assyria. They needed the support of the other small states. However, Ahaz, the king of Judah, was not interested in becoming party to the rebellion. The kings of Syria and Israel decided to take over Judah and put on the throne a king who would be willing to join them. Ahaz, thoroughly alarmed, reacted by calling on the king of Assyria for help. This state of affairs forms the background for much of Isaiah's early preaching.

When Ahaz died almost twenty years later, a new king named Hezekiah came to the throne of Judah. Since the days of Ahaz, the kingdom of Judah had been vassal to Assyria. Hezekiah attempted new religious and political arrangements. However, he made the same mistake as his predecessors. He tried to play the political power game. He and his counselors decided to seek the support of Egypt, Assyria's perennial rival, for anti-Assyrian moves. Isaiah perceived this as a lack of confidence in Yahweh's ability to carry out his own plans for his people. This is what is behind the forceful utterances of Isaiah directed against military preparation and stressing the futility of looking to Egypt for help.

After 705, there is another historical development to which Isaiah addresses himself. A new and powerful king has come to the throne of Assyria. He begins a series of campaigns against his rebellious vassals. Judah is included in his list of accounts to be settled.

Isaiah's tone now changes. Previously, he had spoken loudly and strongly against military engagement. Now the Assyrian king, according to reports in Isaiah, mocked the ability of Yahweh to defend his people against the might of Assyria. Stung by this scornful blasphemy, Isaiah became the inspiration for Jerusalem's resistance against the invaders.

After this, the final years of Isaiah slip into obscurity. A late tradition relates that Isaiah was put to death by Hezekiah's successor, Manasseh, but there is no way to determine the truth of this tradition.

ISAIAH'S CALL

Please read: 6.1-13

Several prophets describe what can be termed their "call experience," their awakening to awareness of a special mission from Yahweh to be his spokesman. The call description usually reveals the basic insight and message of the prophet. Isaiah presents his call in terms of a vision of Yahweh in the Temple.

Isaiah is standing in the Temple, looking toward the Holy of Holies, the front room of the Temple which contained the Ark of the Covenant and was considered the special place of Yahweh's presence.

As he looks, he "sees" Yahweh whose cloak fills the whole Temple. Around Yahweh are seraphim, beings part human and part animal or bird belonging to the religious symbolism of the time and associated with Yahweh as part of the heavenly court. The seraphim sing of the holiness of Yahweh.

"Holy, holy, holy is the LORD of hosts!
All the earth is filled with his glory!"

The song of the seraphim is accompanied by a trembling of the Temple itself and the building is filled with smoke.

This scene points to a great characteristic of Yahweh, his holiness. Yahweh is holy, which is to say he is different from the creation he has made. Against the weakness, mortality, limitation of his creatures stand the power, life and immense power of Yahweh. Against the sinfulness of his creatures stands the goodness of Yahweh.

Overwhelmed by this experience of the holiness of Yahweh, Isaiah acknowledges his own mortality and weakness and the mortality and weakness of the people of whom he is part. He cries out, "Woe is me, I am doomed!" Being in the presence of indescribable goodness and power almost crushes the man who now becomes frighteningly aware of his own frailty.

As the vision continues, one of the seraphim takes a coal from the small altar in the Temple on which incense is burning and touches it to Isaiah's lips. By this symbolic gesture, Isaiah is made to realize that Yahweh has cleansed and purifed him.

Next Isaiah depicts Yahweh in conversation with a heavenly court. "Whom shall I send?" Yahweh asks. Isaiah volunteers. "Here I am . . . send me!"

Isaiah is assured that he will indeed carry Yahweh's message to the people. However, they will not listen to him. His attempts to stir them to conversion, to return to Yahweh, will result only in their retreating more deeply into their own wishes, their own schemes.

Isaiah asks how long this situation of call to conversion rejected will continue. The appalling response is that it will continue until there is a terrible destruction in the land. However, even in the midst of disaster, there will be some hope. At least some remnant of faithful people will remain to receive and carry on Yahweh's promise.

Key points in Isaiah's call are thus:
1. his deep appreciation of the holiness of Yahwch. This places Yahweh over against the weakness and sinfulness of people and human institutions.
2. the reality of failure. Isaiah's message of repentance will not be received and the people will bring disaster on themselves. However, this disaster does not mean total abandonment by God. There is hope for the future.

INGRATITUDE AND EMPTY RELIGION

Please read: 1.2-17

Isaiah voices Yahweh's indictment of his people. He has made them his sons but they have disowned him. The people of Judah do not even have the sense of dumb animals. The ox and donkey at least know their owners and depend on them. The people seem completely oblivious to the reality, not that Yahweh owns them in some crass and degrading sense but that he has made them for himself and only in fidelity to him can they be what they wish to be.

Various catastrophes have wasted the land. These should have shown the people the foolishness of trusting in passing things but they still remain blind and deaf to the truth. Through it all, the charade of ritual continues unabated. Isaiah condemns these empty gestures of sacrifice and religious celebration. All is meaningless without true reform of life.

"Cease doing evil; learn to do good.
Make justice your aim: redress the wronged,
hear the orphan's plea, defend the widow."

ANOTHER EXPRESSION OF INGRATITUDE

Please read: 5.1-7

Isaiah uses what was probably a popular song to convey his view of Judah. The song, as he recites it, was about a vineyard and all that the owner of the vineyard had done to make it strong, healthy, fruitful. He had planted it on a hillside, spaded the ground well, removed the rocks and now waited for the grapes to grow. But despite the care, only wild, sour grapes grew on the vines. There was no further point in the owner working on the vineyard. The only sensible thing to do was to let it revert to wilderness.

After calling on the people of Jerusalem and Judah to approve the grower's course of action, Isaiah comes to his point.

"The vineyard of the LORD is the house of Israel,
and the men of Judah are his cherished plant;
He looked for judgment, but see, bloodshed!
for justice, but hark, the outcry!"

His loving care had produced not lives faithful to the covenant but the shedding of innocent blood and the outcries of the oppressed against their oppressors.

CORRUPTION AND INJUSTICE

Please read: 5.8-25

The powerful are busily engaged in increasing their property by all manner of corrupt manipulation. But all they gain will be turned into ruins.

The luxury seekers drink and party. But their parties are soon to end. In their craze for pleasure, they have ignored their God and their brothers. Those who have become so accustomed to delicacies will soon experience hunger and thirst as they are carried off by their enemies.

The depravity of the rich and powerful will soon receive its just punishment. All will come to recognize that God is indeed protector of the poor, the helpless, the faithful, and different from the self-serving standards of the corrupt.

FALSE TRUST

Please read: 31.1-3

Only Yahweh is the Holy One of Israel. Only he is beyond the weakness and limitation of creatures. Only he–no one or nothing else.

Yet instead of trusting in him in the face of the political danger arising from the power of Assyria, the rulers of Judah plot and plan and send ambassadors to Egypt to make alliances for defense.

The treaties and guarantees are less than useless. Trusting in the power of Egypt is a delusion. The intrigues and mutual defense pacts are doomed. Those who trust in Egypt rather than Yahweh will soon discover that they have put their hopes in a paper tiger.

ISAIAH'S MESSAGE IN SIGN: THE NAKEDNESS OF CAPTIVITY

Please read: 20.1-6

Along with the spoken word, the prophets sometimes used signs and gestures to convey their message. They acted out what they were trying to say.

This kind of symbolic action is not strange to us. Recall protests against war or the neutron bomb in which people with black armbands walked through city streets carrying coffins symbolic of those who had been or would be killed in warfare. Or think of the demonstrations in which people have worn chains around their bodies as graphic reminders of the lack of freedom of people behind the Iron Curtain and elsewhere. Isaiah performs such a dramatic gesture.

Enemy Assyrian armies are near Judah. The people are pinning their hope for deliverance from this threat on help expected to come from Egypt.

Isaiah's behavior serves as a warning.

Prisoners were usually marched off into captivity or exile naked. For some time, Isaiah has been very scantily dressed. The point of his peculiar behavior now becomes clear. Just as Isaiah has appeared publicly in humiliating near-nakedness, so will the forces of Egypt, on which the people of Judah are relying, be carried off into captivity in obvious and public degradation.

ISAIAH'S MESSAGE TO OTHER NATIONS

Please read: *10.5-19*

In Isaiah's view, Yahweh was the only God who counted in the universe. All events fitted into his plans. He could use Assyria, a far-away land, to carry out his purposes. He was using it—as a rod with which to chastise his sinful and ungrateful people.

However, Assyria was interpreting its victories in a boastful and self-aggrandizing way. It saw all that was happening simply as the result of its own military ferocity. It saw Israel and Judah as no different from all the other lands it had overrun. It believed Yahweh to be the same powerless nonentity as the gods of other nations whose temples had been reduced to rubble.

Assyria fails to see itself as it is, an instrument in the hands of the all-powerful and holy Yahweh. It is like an axe which speaks as if it alone were responsible for chopping. Assyria will learn through experience that Yahweh is the "Holy One of Israel." The disasters that befall it will be the result of its blindness to the fact that its strength has been the arm of Yahweh. Yahweh has allowed the Assyrians to conquer and despoil his people and their land because he wants them to return to their trust in him. Assyria has failed totally to recognize this and is guilty of self-deception in seeing its power as its own creation.

ISAIAH AND IMMANUEL

In the prophecies of Isaiah, there appears someone who receives the name, "Immanuel," "God-with-us." The prophecies focus on the emergence of some individual (individuals?) from whom great things are expected for Jerusalem and Judah. These passages come to play a great role in the Christian understanding of Jesus, so we shall consider them in some detail.

THE BIRTH OF THE CHILD

Please read: 7.1-17

The time is about 735. The king of Israel and the king of Damascus (Syria), set on rebellion against Assyria, are marching on Judah. Its king, Ahaz, refuses to take part in their uprising. The approach of the enemy armies has been reported and Ahaz is on a tour of inspection of the walls of Jerusalem. The fall of his city will almost certainly mean his own death and the execution of all in his family when the rebel kings make someone more sympathetic to their purposes ruler in Jerusalem.

Isaiah goes out to meet the troubled king while he is inspecting the city defenses. Isaiah delivers a message of consolation. He tells Ahaz not to be afraid of the two kings who are marching against him. The countries they rule will be destroyed in a short time. Isaiah calls on Ahaz to put his total trust in Yahweh in this trying period.
"Unless your faith is firm
you shall not be firm!"

To stiffen the back of the fearful Ahaz, Isaiah makes what sounds like a daring offer. He invites Ahaz to "Ask for a sign from the LORD, your God; let it be deep as the nether world, or high as the sky!"

A word on signs. A sign in the Bible is not necessarily something wonderful or spectacular. In fact, most often, it is not something of this character. It is regularly a saying or action presented along with the message of the prophet to illustrate and strengthen the force of that message. So, for example, the incident we read previously of Isaiah's going about almost naked as a symbol that the Egyptians would be taken naked into captivity is called by the same name, a sign. Here, Isaiah has invited the king to ask for some kind of act, not necessarily miraculous, that would offer encouragement and support.

Ahaz appears to throw up his hands in pious horror at the idea of bargaining with Yahweh. "I will not ask! I will not tempt the LORD!"

Isaiah's reaction makes it clear that there is nothing pious about Ahaz's answer. Ahaz will not ask for a sign because he has already made up his mind about where he will go for help. He has already appealed to the king of Assyria to send a relief army. Ahaz has no intention of trusting in Yahweh.

In exasperation, Isaiah responds that it is bad enough for Ahaz to be stubborn and difficult with him. It is quite something else for Ahaz to be stubborn and difficult with God. And note how Isaiah has called Yahweh "your God" in speaking to Ahaz but now takes that back and calls him "my God" (v.11). Ahaz's lack of faith amounts to a rejection of Yahweh as the saving God for him and his people.

Isaiah affirms that Yahweh will give a sign nonetheless. Remember again the meaning of "sign." Not necessarily, or even usually, something miraculous, but some act or event that supports or emphasizes or illustrates a prophetic message. 7.14 gives the sign. "The *almah* shall be with child, and bear a son, and shall name him Immanuel."

Here we encounter some rough sledding. The Hebrew word *almah* is translated in the New American Bible as "virgin." More correctly, the word means a young woman until the birth of her first child or a girl of marriageable age. There is nothing in the passage that points to virginal conception, to a young woman having a child outside the normal process of conception.

The conception and birth of the child to the young woman and the name given to that child, Immanuel or God-with-us, will be a call, a challenge, to trust in the presence of God with his people. At the same time, a refusal to respond in faith to this challenge will bring disaster on Jerusalem and Judah. Thus, the sign is also a threat.

Trust in Yahweh will be rewarded by deliverance from the danger posed by the invading kings. Failure to trust will end in the land being reduced to a state of wilderness.

The king's decision betrays his lack of trust. He places all his confidence in the help of Assyria rather than in the saving power of Yahweh. He has broken covenant with Yahweh. His rash, unfaithful action has doomed his city and his country. This remains true even if the present danger of invasion will collapse.

Who is the child who will be born and be given the name Immanuel? Unfortunately his identity remains a mystery to us. The sign must have meant something to the people to whom it was directed. For the sign to make any sense, the woman and child must have been identifiable. Many solutions to the riddle have been offered.

Some scholars hold that the sign is the birth of Hezekiah, the son of Ahaz. The family of Ahaz is in danger of destruction. The birth of a son to the wife of Ahaz would show Yahweh's protection of the line of the family of David.

Others hold that the child is a son of Isaiah whose birth will be a sign of God's presence. Other sons of Isaiah with symbolic names are mentioned in 7.3 and 8.1-4. There we meet "A remnant will remain" and "Quick spoils, speedy plunder."

However, these suggestions, and all of the many others offered, run into various difficulties so that the actual historical identity of the child cannot be known with certainty.

The aspect of wonder and intervention of Yahweh that surrounds this passage leaves it open to deeper understanding and interpretation as time goes on. By the time of the writing of the Gospels, the birth of Jesus of the Virgin Mary is seen as the fulfillment of Isaiah's sign (Matthew 1.23).

IMMANUEL: THE GREAT KING

Please read: 9.1-6

This passage probably belongs to the same period as the one just discussed. Shortly after 735, the Assyrians did invade and conquer the northern provinces of the kingdom of Israel. The question now was, "Has Israel been abandoned by Yahweh?" "Is its life over, or will it again thrive under a king like David?"

This passage speaks of hope for the future. The people in the darkness of conquest and oppression will again be liberated through the power of Yahweh who is faithful to his people. There will also be a king like David to rule when Yahweh has restored his people.

It was the custom of the time to give throne names to a new king. Titles conveying what he would be and do were assigned to the king on the day of his installation or to the future king on the day of his birth. As might be expected, these names described the king in grandiose terms. The child in this passage is either an heir-apparent to the throne who has been born in Jerusalem or one whose birth is expected in the near future.

His throne names are catalogued. He is "Wonder-Counselor," the one who needs no help or advice from others since Yahweh himself guides his thoughts. He is "God-Hero." The king in Jerusalem was considered an adopted son of Yahweh. He was Yahweh's representative on earth. He is "Father-Forever" and "Prince of Peace." He will rule the kingdom of David in fidelity to Yahweh and his covenant. All of this will happen because of the constant presence of Yahweh to his people.

Once again, these words reflect the exalted hope for a king who would be the true and faithful representative of God on earth and usher in a period of peace and prosperity.

THE GREAT KING

Please read: 11.1-9

Isaiah, fired by his unwavering trust in Yahweh, gives voice once more to expectation for a king in whom the power, goodness and holiness of Yahweh will be obvious. A king will come from the "stump of Jesse," i.e., the family of David.

The spirit of Yahweh, his life, his power, will fill this king. This will manifest itself in the way the king lives and rules. He will embody all those qualities that go to make an ideal ruler, one truly formed according to the goodness of Yahweh. All the virtues of the great men of Israel's history will come together in him. He will be wise and understanding, so that he can settle cases and situations in the best interests of all concerned. He will be prudent and brave in caring for his people.

All this will reach its high point in the fact that the guiding principle of all the king does will be "the fear of the LORD," an appreciation of Yahweh and the kind of God he is.

The results of this kind of rule will be obvious. Injustice and oppression will disappear from the land. The king will be outfitted not with weapons and armor but with the truth and fidelity to Yahweh.

Because of this, the land will prosper and rejoice. The general well-being is summed up in the image of the "peaceable kingdom." Natural enemies will live in harmony with one another; the wolf and the lamb, the leopard and the kid, the calf and the lion. All the land will be "filled with knowledge of the LORD." All creation will experience Yahweh's power and goodness.

Isaiah had some king in the line of David in mind. Possibly he was thinking of some son of the king who had already been born and would soon ascend the throne.

However, a sense of wonder and great expectation pervades this text and the previous two we have read. As king after actual king failed to live up to the great hopes expressed, it was not strange that there would develop more and more a sense of waiting for a king who would in some special way fulfill these promises. The uniqueness attributed to that king became more pronounced over the years.

When Christians struggled to find ways to express their belief in Jesus, it is easy to understand how they took these passages from their Scriptures and saw in them early descriptions of God's work through Jesus.

ANOTHER ORACLE OF HOPE

Please read: 2.1-5

Here is another promise of universal peace. The picture is that of a procession of people from all over the world coming to Jerusalem, to Mount Zion on the eastern side of the city. The Temple stood on this mountain. At the Temple, all nations learn the true way of life from Yahweh, the God of Israel. Because of this, all peoples come to live at peace with one another. The instruments of war are refashioned into tools for the peaceful pursuit of agriculture.

"They shall beat their swords into plowshares
and their spears into pruning hooks."

THE MESSAGE OF ISAIAH

Holiness is the characteristic of Yahweh that is always in the forefront for Isaiah. Yahweh lives beyond the frailty, sinfulness, limitation, corruption of humans. He is the powerful protector and guide of his people. He is the good defender of the dignity of the poor, the weak, the defenseless. In the light of his truth, hypocritical religious practice stands out in harsh and vivid outline for all to see.

The people of Jerusalem and Judah have twisted their relationship to the "Holy One of Israel," as Isaiah so often calls Yahweh. They have put their trust in political and military alliances. They oppress the weak and helpless among them for their own gain. They keep up the trappings of religion without facing the implications that an honest relationship with God has for conduct toward others. They are bringing disaster on themselves. Their city and their land will be destroyed. They will lose freedom and ill-gotten prosperity.

However, their pain is not the vengeance of a vindictive God. Rather in the loss of what they have, they will come once more to trust in Yahweh. Yahweh will never abandon his people, no matter what happens. Sometime in the future a king will finally come who will be the man after Yahweh's heart. He will govern in justice, integrity and fidelity to Yahweh. One day, nations will live in peace because all will be governed by the peace-bringing will of Yahweh, the Holy One.

SUGGESTIONS FOR REFLECTION

1. Which of the prophets previously mentioned does Isaiah's warning against political maneuvering resemble?

2. Read Isaiah 1.2-17, Isaiah 5.1-7, and Isaiah 5.8-25 again, to locate passages in each that emphasize the themes of: holiness of Yahweh, the sinfulness of the people and human institutions, and the impending disaster.

3. The Israelites in the days of Isaiah put their trust alternately in their neighbors, Egypt and Assyria, to be their strength and protection in their own powerlessness, instead of in Yahweh. How do we do the same thing today in our personal lives? Give an example.

4. "Why does Yahweh let his own chosen ones suffer and his enemies prosper?" You will often hear this question when people look at life. How did Isaiah answer this question when the Israelites, the chosen ones, were being plundered by the Assyrians, the enemies of Yahweh?

5. Explain how holy people of the Scriptures could ask God for a "sign" of his will, without being superstitious or desiring a miracle.

6. The story of Ahaz is a challenge to radical trust in Yahweh over earthly princes. If you had been faced with Ahaz's condition and dilemma, how would you have responded? Is there anything in your own life history of dilemma-solving which could let you see your own pattern?

7. How does the passage, Isaiah 9.5 add to our understanding of the Hebrew concept of a name? To a king's name and identity especially?

8. In the "peaceable kingdom" natural enemies will live in harmony with one another. What would a peaceable kingdom look like in the world today? our own country today? your city, family, today? In you today? What

seems to be in the way of it at present? Could the obstacles be broken down?

9. Give three examples from the writing of Isaiah that new hope is often symbolized in prophesy about a newborn baby, or child. Why is this a good symbol for hope?'

10. Why do all, even the religious people, come under Isaiah's prophesy of disaster?

11. Why is the book of Isaiah divided by most scholars? After reading this section about the message of Isaiah 1–39, what are the main themes treated by this prophet?

CHAPTER VI

JEREMIAH AND THE BURDEN OF CARRYING GOD'S WORD

JEREMIAH: HIS TIMES

As was the case with Isaiah, the preaching of Jeremiah covers a span of about forty troubled years. Jeremiah came from a small village a few miles northeast of Jerusalem. He was born during the last years of the reign of the king, Manasseh.

This king was notorious, according to the notice in 2 Kings 21.1-18. "Manasseh . . . did evil in the sight of the LORD, following the abominable practices of the nations . . . He worshiped and served the whole host of heaven . . . He immolated his son by fire. He practiced soothsaying and divination and reintroduced the consulting of ghosts and spirits. He did much evil in the LORD's sight and provoked him to anger . . . Then the LORD spoke through his servants the prophets: 'Because Manasseh, king of Judah, has practiced these abominations and has done greater evil than all that was done by the Amorites before him and has led Judah into sin by his idols, therefore says the LORD, the God of Israel: "I will bring such evil on Jerusalem and Judah that, wherever anyone hears of it, his ears will ring . . . " ' In addition to the sin which he caused Judah to commit, Manasseh did evil in the sight of the LORD, shedding so much innocent blood as to fill the length and breadth of Jerusalem."

Jeremiah's boyhood years were lived in the shadow of this situation. While Manasseh ruled, the kingdom of Judah remained under the control of Assyria. This political control included the acceptance of the gods worshiped by the Assyrians. The local gods of Canaan could also be found in the official religious line-up in Jerusalem. The people of Jerusalem saw and honored gods aplenty.

As usual, as the relationship of the people with their God decayed, so did the way the people treated each other. Injustice and violence became more and more accepted ways of life.

The first stage of Jeremiah's preaching began in the year 627 B.C. At that time, there had been a different king of Judah for about 13 years. His name was Josiah. A grandson of Manasseh, he had been installed as king in 640. Since he was only eight years old when he became king, the kingdom was ruled by regents. During these years, nothing changed. The evil times of Manasseh continued. In 627, Josiah was a man of 21. When Jeremiah came on the scene, he was about the same age.

JEREMIAH'S CALL

Please read: 1.4-14

Jeremiah describes his perception of his mission in terms of a dialogue begun by Yahweh.

The God of Israel tells Jeremiah that he has destined him for a special task. Yahweh has set him apart to speak in his name, not only to Jerusalem and Judah but also to the nations like Egypt and Assyria whose actions so often determined the fate of Judah.

Jeremiah wants none of this. He objects on the grounds of his youth and the lack of ability to speak impressively that would usually be associated with youth.

Yahweh overrules Jeremiah. Jeremiah's inadequacies are not at issue. Yahweh is the one who is sending him. In the face of opposition and danger, he is not to be afraid because Yahweh will be with him. The commission to Jeremiah to speak in Yahweh's name is made even more pointed.
"See, I place my words in your mouth."
The role of prophet as spokesman for God could not be clearer.

The threatening character of Jeremiah's message is all too obvious. He will "root up, tear down, destroy, demolish." This fundamental description of vocation is carried further in the next verses.

First, there is a play on words. Jeremiah sees, if not in an actual walk through a garden at least in his mind's eye, the branch of a tree. In his internal conversation with Yahweh, he hears the question, "What do you see?" Jeremiah responds that he sees the branch of *shaqed,* "an almond tree." This suggests the word, *shoqed*–"watching." In this simple exchange, the truth strikes Jeremiah. Yahweh is *watching* over the word he will speak through Jeremiah and will make it happen.

Once more, either in reality or in imagination, Jeremiah sees a pot steaming over a fire. The pot is tipped so that boiling water is spilling out from north to south.

This device puts the future of his country and people vividly before Jeremiah. As the boiling water spills from north to south, so will evil boil over from north to south for his homeland. Although not all details are certain, disaster will surely come upon Judah and Jerusalem through an invasion by powerful neighbors to the north.

THE FIRST PERIOD OF JEREMIAH'S PREACHING

We can, with reasonable assurance, attach parts of Jeremiah's preaching to various historical situations in the life of the prophet and his country. The first six chapters of the book belong to the early years of Jeremiah's ministry, lasting from about 627 to 622.

The young Josiah is king. He is concerned with the religious and social life of his land. He has sparked some efforts at reform. However, a real force and direction to his reform is not yet established.

Jeremiah's message during this period centers on two points:
1. Judah and Jerusalem must reform.
2. Their sinfulness makes very real the threat of an invasion from the north which would be Yahweh's punishment for infidelity.

THE INFIDELITY OF JUDAH

Please read: 2.1-32

Jeremiah's preaching begins with a note of anguish. He looks back to the period of the wandering in the desert after the departure from Egypt. With a kind of wistful nostalgia, Yahweh remembers those days when his people, totally dependent on him for their survival in the wilderness, remained faithful to him as their only hope. For his part, Yahweh protected his people from any harm or attack.

In vv. 4 and following, the ingratitude of the people is presented in all its starkness. Yahweh asks his people where they have found him at fault. In their new situation of prosperity in the land he gave them, all, even the priests, have forgotten their God and the love and care he showered on them. Even the pagans remain faithful to the nonentities they call gods. But Judah has preferred to run after these nothings despite its experiences of Yahweh.

The punishment is foretold in vv. 14-19. Judah will be prisoner of Egypt and Assyria. This captivity is inevitable because of Judah's abandonment of the only true source of its life and help, Yahweh.

Judah's guilt is vividly portrayed in vv. 20-24. The classic stance of sinfulness is put into those awful words, "I will not serve."

There are references to pagan religious practices and shrines, "on every high hill, under every green tree, you gave yourself to harlotry." The "high places" and trees were especially associated with the worship of the nature gods that so attracted the people of Judah. Judah is like a camel in heat, panting after false gods. Judah is willing to call a wooden idol "father," and a stone statue "the one who gave me birth." Yet, when disaster threatens, Judah remembers Yahweh again and goes back to him. But now it is too late. Let those wooden and stone gods help if they can.

THE CALL TO REPENTANCE

Please read: 3.19-25; 4.1-4

Yahweh's plan for his people was to treat them as sons, to give them all that would show his tender concern for them. He had hoped that Judah would call him "My Father" and live out this loving relationship. This was not to be.

Yet, the invitation to return still stands. All the people need do is to turn again to Yahweh. If this happens, they will experience again the signs of Yahweh's gracious and saving presence.

PUNISHMENT THREATENED: INVASION FROM THE NORTH

Please read: 6.1-8, 22-26

Jeremiah raises the alarm in and around Jerusalem. The people must flee. An awesome army is on the march from the north. Beautiful Jerusalem will be surrounded by hostile armies. Each enemy king will plunder at will. And all of this comes from Jerusalem's wickedness.

The invading horde is cruel and pitiless, armed with bow and javelin. The noise it makes is that of a roaring sea. As it approaches, it will not be safe to go out of doors. Destruction is on the move!

JEREMIAH'S SILENCE DURING A PERIOD OF REFORM

In the year 621, the king Josiah began a thoroughgoing reform. He smashed the pagan idols and their shrines. He reinstated the pure worship of Yahweh. The corrupting ties with foreign lands were cut.

Strangely enough, Jeremiah, the preacher of reform, does not seem to receive any kind of recognition. Nor does he seem to have become part of the reform movement. At least, we have no evidence that he did. However, he certainly approved the plans and actions of Josiah. For the rest of Josiah's life and reign, Jeremiah appears to have remained quietly in the background.

THE FAILURE OF REFORM: JEREMIAH ONCE MORE IN ACTION–THE TEMPLE SERMON

Please read: 7.1-15; 26.1-19

For almost 20 years, Josiah fostered devotion to Yahweh and rooted out pagan practices. This ended abruptly when, in 609, he was killed in an ill-advised battle against an Egyptian army. Shortly after the unfortunate death of Josiah, the Egyptians took *de facto* control of Jerusalem and installed as king a son of Josiah named Jehoiakim. There was no doubt that the Egyptians intended this man to be their puppet.

It became obvious under Jehoiakim that Josiah's reform had accomplished mainly a cosmetic benefit. On the surface, reform seemed to have been effective, but beneath the enforced house-cleaning, the attraction to religious perversion, to immorality and to injustice remained as strong as ever.

Jeremiah emerged from his obscurity. Chapters 7–20 give a good sample of his activity during the reign of Jehoiakim.

A dramatic confrontation took place in the year 608 on the steps of the Temple. The passages indicated for reading are two accounts of the same incident.

Crowds push through the Temple courtyards on a feast day. Jeremiah shoves his way to a spot from which he can be seen and heard. He accuses the jostling throng of making a mockery of the religious ritual by the evil of their lives. With great confidence, they carry out the prescribed rites for prayer and sacrifice. But when the ritual is done, they return to stealing, murder, adultery, perjury, worship of false gods.

Jeremiah condemns this hypocrisy for what it is. If the people rely on the fact that Yahweh is uniquely among them in the Temple, Jeremiah reminds them that this is only by the free choice of Yahweh himself. He can be driven away by evil and infidelity. Jeremiah recalls the story of an ancient sanctuary at Shiloh which had also been sacred to Yahweh but which had been destroyed by the Philistines about 350 years previously. The same fate awaits this Temple in Jerusalem if the people do not reform their lives. The reaction to Jeremiah's boldness is just what might be expected.

Not so long ago, newspapers carried the story of a clergyman disturbed by what he considered the apathy of his congregation. On a Sunday morning, dressed in the most disreputable clothes he could find, he went to his church. With some minor changes in appearance and a liberal application of dirt, he made himself unrecognizable. Before the Sunday service, he pitched himself down in front of the church as if he were in a sick or drunken stupor. Not one of the congregation stopped to help him, or even tried to summon help.

When the congregation was fully assembled, he got up and walked down the aisle to his pulpit. He proceeded to tell his people what they had done. He lost his job almost immediately. Nobody wanted to be made to feel false and guilty.

Jeremiah's hearers took a more radical approach to this troublemaker. The people, and many of their leaders, called for Jeremiah's death for blasphemy. Yahweh would certainly never leave this magnificent Temple and his place among his people, they claimed.

It was only the intervention of some higher minded leaders that prevented Jeremiah's being lynched.

JEREMIAH AGAINST THE KING

Please read: 22.13-19

Jeremiah's convictions about fidelity to Yahweh moved him to confront even the most exalted personages. King Jehoiakim emptied the national treasury to build himself a palace and forced his people to do the work.

Jeremiah accused Jehoiakim of using a false standard of kingship. It was always the ideal of kingship in Israel and

Judah that the king served as servant of Yahweh. His role was to promote justice and integrity and fidelity and so secure the peace and prosperity of his people.

But this king forced the common people, "his neighbors," to work without pay on his personal building project. Jeremiah reminded the self-serving young ruler of his good father, Josiah, and the integrity of his reign. The oppression and extortion of the son are far from the justice of the father.

This too will bring its own harsh penalty. When Jehoiakim dies, there will be no noble and sincere mourning rites. All he can expect is to have his body dragged outside the city where it will receive the "burial of an ass," i.e., be dumped on the garbage heap.

JEREMIAH'S LIFE AS MESSAGE

Please read: 16.1-13

Jeremiah's lifestyle would also teach a lesson.

Marriage and having children was of the utmost importance. But Jeremiah has the conviction that he is not to marry. Why? His own life, barren of wife and children, is a sign to all parents that they might just as well be barren. Their children are going to die in desperate circumstances.

Jeremiah is not to take part in the customary mourning rites that comforted the survivors of the deceased. Why? As a sign that days were coming in which there would be neither the time nor the opportunity to mourn the great numbers of those who would die tragically.

Jeremiah is not to take part in any of the usual homey celebrations that mark the simple and the great joys of life. Why? Because a long harsh silence will muzzle all sounds of joy in the land.

The reason for the tragedy threatened by Jeremiah's strange behavior is the infidelity of the people to their God.

JEREMIAH'S PERSONAL TRAGEDY

Please read: 11.18–12.6; 15.10-20; 17.14-18; 18.18-23; 20.7-18

These passages, often called the "Confessions of Jeremiah," are unique in the preserved sayings of the prophets. They give the closest look at the personal attitude of one prophet toward what he felt compelled by divine call to do.

Jeremiah carried a heavy burden. He had to preach the destruction of his own people. He had to endure scorn and self-doubt when his threats failed to materialize. He was hated by many because of the threat he posed to their way of life. This hatred led, more than once, to attempts on his life.

The Confessions of Jeremiah, often borrowing from the language of the Psalms, express his deepest feelings. He complains to Yahweh about what he must go through. He calls on Yahweh for vindication, not so much for himself but for Yahweh's message which he speaks. Yahweh's own people are standing against the way of reform to which Yahweh is summoning them.

Jeremiah's language sometimes sounds vindictive.
"So now, deliver their children to famine,
do away with them by the sword.
Let their wives be made childless and widows!
let their men die of pestilence,
their young men be slain by the sword in battle." (18.21)

To see only a bitter cry for revenge in such words would be to miss the point. Yahweh's word has called to conversion. Yahweh's word is meant for good. To reject that good word can only bring disaster and grief. Jeremiah calls for the fulfillment of Yahweh's word.

Sometimes the responses that Jeremiah receives to his outcries are less than reassuring. On one occasion, after a passionate lament, Jeremiah perceives Yahweh's response as:
"If running against men has wearied you,
how will you run against horses?" (12.5)
In other words, Jeremiah is told, "If you think that the situations you have had to face have been painful, you haven't seen anything yet." Beyond this, is the call to faith, to trust in Yahweh despite the suffering and the apparent failure.

Jeremiah is also aware, in crisis situations, of a renewal of his vocation with its promise of help from Yahweh. In words that echo his call experience, Jeremiah understands Yahweh's message.
"I will make you toward this people a solid wall of brass.
Though they fight against you, they shall not prevail,
For I am with you, to deliver and rescue you, says the LORD.
I will free you from the hand of the wicked,
and rescue you from the grasp of the violent." (15.20)

Jeremiah did not relish his mission of condemning his own people. He hoped eagerly for their return to a sincere relationship with Yahweh. He believed that this would insure peace, justice and security in the land.

But few paid attention. For forty long years he was ridiculed, rejected, harshly treated, even physically attacked. A prose account of some of the conflict and suffering of Jeremiah, dictated to his secretary Baruch, can be found in 36.1–45.5.

He had to struggle through all of this just as any of us would. He felt deep anguish. He cried out to Yahweh to release him from his mission or to show the truth of what he had been preaching.

Perhaps the vocation of a prophet is best summed up in these vivid words of Jeremiah.
"I say to myself, I will not mention him,
I will speak in his name no more.
But then it becomes like fire burning in my heart,
imprisoned in my bones;
I grow weary holding it in,
I cannot endure it." (20.9)

JEREMIAH AND THE LAST YEARS OF JERUSALEM AND JUDAH

The complicated political history of the Kingdom of Judah continued after its submission to Egypt in 609. A new power in the north, Babylonia, was stretching its greedy fingers toward Palestine. By 604, change was in the air. Jehoiakim, the king at Jerusalem, switched his allegiance from Egypt to Nebuchadnezzar, the king of this new power.

However, the desire for independence, not too difficult to understand, kept asserting itself. Plots and intrigues flourished. In 601, Jehoiakim thought the time ripe to declare his independence of the Babylonians.

This was a mistake. Nebuchadnezzar dispatched punitive expeditions that hacked away at the exposed flanks of Judah. In 598, a full-scale invasion was launched from Babylonia. Just as the campaign began, Jehoiakim died. Whether this was a convenient coincidence or assassination is not known. At any rate, his eighteen-year-old son succeeded him. Within three months, Jerusalem surrendered to the Babylonians.

Nebuchadnezzar carried off as booty many of the treasures of Jerusalem and Judah. He sent as prisoners to Babylonia the leaders and the better educated among the population. However, he allowed the kingdom of Judah to go on with a man named Zedekiah as king.

The next ten years, from 597 to 587, witness more of what had gone on before. There is no end of plot and counter-plot in the maneuvering for complete liberation of Judah.

JEREMIAH AND THE FAILURES OF LEADERSHIP

Please read: 23

During this period of conspiracy, Jeremiah addresses himself once again to what he sees as the tragedy of his land. First of all, Jeremiah is critical of the rule of kings whose short-sighted policies bring only harm to their people (23. 1-2).

Jeremiah is especially harsh on the prophets, the people who, like himself, claimed to speak in Yahweh's name. These people, who were to speak Yahweh's truth, misled the people by their own corrupt lives and by the preaching of lies. Their message does not come from Yahweh but from their own self and nation-serving wishes. They especially seem to be guilty of proclaiming soothing words, words which do not call the people to repentance, words which encourage hopes for independence through rebellion. According to Jeremiah, this is not the time for comforting words. The conduct of the king and the people has earned for them the harsh judgment of their God. The true spokesman for Yahweh at this time will try to turn the people from their evil ways. Prophets who have really stood in the presence of Yahweh would "proclaim to my people my words. They would have brought them back from evil ways and from their wicked deeds" (v. 22).

THE FUTILITY OF REBELLION AND CONFLICT WITH ANOTHER PROPHET

Please read: 27.1–28.17

The year is 594. The chefs of rebellion are busily stirring the pot. Ambassadors from several small states around Judah that are also subject to Babylonia have gathered in Jerusalem to make plans for rebellion.

All this furor is being supported by men claiming to be prophets. They say, "You need not serve the king of Babylon" (27.9, 14). These false prophets are also claiming that the sacred vessels which the Babylonians had stolen from the Temple in 597 would soon be returned in the caravans of returning exiles brought back by Yahweh (27.16).

Onto this fever for resistance based on false hope, Jeremiah throws the cold water of his message. In Yahweh's name, he promises, "I have given all these lands into the hand of Nebuchadnezzar, king of Babylon, my servant . . . if any nation or kingdom will not serve Nebuchadnezzar, king of Babylon, or will not bend its neck under the yoke of the king of Babylon, I will punish that nation with sword, famine, and pestilence, says the LORD, until I give them into his hand" (27.5-8).

But Jeremiah is not the only one claiming to speak for Yahweh.

In a symbolic gesture, Jeremiah had made for himself the kind of yoke that was tied about an ox's neck. This yoke was meant to dramatize the truth that Judah and the other nations were to remain under the yoke on Babylon until

Yahweh's plans were accomplished. Another man, also accepted as a prophet, Hananiah, disputes Jeremiah's message. The message he claims to have from Yahweh is, "I will break the yoke of the king of Babylon" (28.4). He promises that within two years, the exiles that had been carried off to Babylonia with their king will return. When Jeremiah contradicts the pronouncement of Hananiah, Hananiah displays his own symbolic gesture. He breaks the yoke on Jeremiah's neck! "Thus says the LORD: 'Even so, within two years I will break the yoke of the Nebuchadnezzar, king of Babylon, from off the neck of all the nations' " (28.11).

It seems that Jeremiah is left startled or puzzled by this turn of events. The text simply records that "the prophet Jeremiah went away."

Later, Jeremiah apparently received reassurance. He went to Hananiah and told him that though he was able to break the wooden yoke, he would never break the iron yoke which represented the rule of Nebuchadnezzar and was Yahweh's will at this time. And because Hananiah has prophesied falsehood, he will suffer the fate of a false prophet, death.

This curious incident brings us face to face, in a dramatic way, with a very real problem. How can people know which person or persons, claiming to speak in God's name, actually do so? The recent experience with the self-styled messiah in Guyana, and the presence of others like him, makes this a crucial question. The answer is not easy to come by.

It is interesting to note that Jeremiah gives what he considers one characteristic of a true prophet. "From of old, the prophets who were before you and me prophesied war, woe, and pestilence against many lands and mighty kingdoms. But the prophet who prophesies peace is recognized as truly sent by the LORD only when his prophetic prediction is fulfilled" (28.8-9).

In other words, according to Jeremiah, the most characteristic role of the prophet is to warn the people of their sins, to call them to repentance, to warn them of the disasters that their sinfulness brings on themselves.

JEREMIAH WRITES TO THE EXILES IN BABYLONIA

Please read: 29.1-15

There is another act of Jeremiah dating to the year 594. Those taken into exile in Babylonia in 597 have been there now for a few years. What does the future hold for them?

Jeremiah sends them an unusual message. He tells them to build houses, to plant gardens, to make arrangements for the marriage of their sons and daughters. They will not be returning home soon. They must settle into their new land and make the necessary provisions for their survival.

THE END OF THE STORY

Jeremiah's message, as expected, did not prove popular. Not many took it seriously. The illusion of freedom won through rebellion captured the imagination of the ruling classes and others.

In 589, the kingdom of Judah revolted against Babylon. Babylonian reaction was not long in coming. Armies invaded Judah and captured its fortified cities one by one. By January 588, Jerusalem itself was besieged. The siege was broken only briefly by the arrival of an Egyptian relief army. This army was sent quickly on its way by Nebuchadnezzar's forces and Jerusalem was once again surrounded and cut off. Though the city held out for a year, its situation was hopeless. In July 587, Jerusalem fell. This time accounts were rendered with a heavy hand. The king, Zedekiah, was forced to watch the execution of his sons. With this bloody sight as his last visual memory, he was blinded and carried off in chains. There was something of a bloodbath in Jerusalem. Many were put into the long lines marching into exile in Babylonia. Jerusalem was destroyed, as were the other cities of Judah. The kingdom of Judah was reduced to a small rural region with a population made up mainly of poor farmers.

Evidently the Babylonians had heard of Jeremiah's efforts to prevent the rebellion. He was allowed to remain in Judah. The Babylonians attempted to set up a government headed by local people, but some hotheads assassinated the new governor and the small Babylonian garrison left behind. Fearing retaliation, some of the populace still left in Judah fled to Egypt for refuge. Jeremiah tried very hard to change their minds but the fear was too great. They migrated to Egypt taking Jeremiah with them.

The last we hear of this troubled prophet he is preaching against a new kind of infidelity developing in Egypt. The people were worshiping false gods even there! It seems that Jeremiah was no more successful there than he had been in Judah.

JEREMIAH AND CONSOLATION

Please read: 30.1–31.40

Till now, our reading of Jeremiah has subjected us to a relentless torrent of sorrow and disaster. Jeremiah was overcome by a sense of doom about his people and great personal suffering. But his message was not without hope.

These two chapters are a collection of Jeremiah's sayings from various times and situations with some possible additions by later editors. These passages point to the constant love and fidelity of Yahweh to his people and the kind of future that that love and fidelity intends even in the midst of tragedy.

The sayings promise, among other things,
salvation from tribulation (30.5-7)
liberation from captivity (30.8-9)
return from the exile (30.10-11)
restoration and new life in the familiar terms of the covenant, "You shall be my people and I will be your God." (30.16-22)
the continuing love of Yahweh which assures restoration of the northern kingdom of Israel destroyed in 721 (30. 2-6).

The most noteworthy of these sayings is the promise of a *"new covenant"* (31.31-34).

Jeremiah's experience of the movement toward reform among his people was not one which offered much hope. For forty years, he and his message of repentance and fidelity to Yahweh was rejected by most of his compatriots. Jeremiah summed up his experience in these words:
"Can the Ethiopian change his skin? the leopard his spots?
As easily would you be able to do good,
accustomed as you are to evil" (13.23).
Jeremiah found himself driven to the terrible conclusion that conversion, renewal, repentance, were beyond his people. They could no more turn from the evil in their lives than the Ethiopian could change his skin or the leopard his spots.

But this insight into the inherent weakness of being human did not drive Jeremiah to despair. Rather, it led him to affirm in even more challenging terms the gracious goodness of Yahweh.

It was true that his people, by their own strength and power, could not change their lives. But what is impossible to human frailty is not impossible to a loving God.

The old covenant showed the people how to live in fidelity to Yahweh. But that way of life remained a command, a rule. It showed the good life but could not help to live that good life. Experience proved that it was a goal beyond reach.

Now there would be a new situation. Yahweh himself would intervene. His good way of life would no longer be an external law but a power, a force vitally alive within the very being of his people. By making his way of life such an integral part of each individual, he would make sure that the new situation between him and his people would not be broken again. The relationship, "I will be your God and you will be my people," will last forever.

THE MESSAGE OF JEREMIAH

Jeremiah's preaching is of such sustained grief and sorrow that word-makers have given his name to any lamentation or "prolonged dolorous utterance." They call such a speech a "jeremiad."

And there is no doubt that for forty years Jeremiah called for a conversion which never materialized with real depth or sincerity. The sometimes blatant, sometimes subtle, infidelity to Yahweh which he saw all around him could lead only to disaster for the nation and its people.

Jeremiah had a deep sense of the goodness of Yahweh, from whom alone could come peace and security. Any other roads led away from what the people were seeking.

Ridiculed for his message, persecuted for the challenge he offered to the set ways of others, tormented by what he believed would be the fate of his beloved people and land, Jeremiah's life was a personal tragedy. As we have seen, even his last words are spoken in Egypt, a land to which he has unwillingly been dragged, against still another treachery on the part of his people. His words seem truly to have been written on the wind.

Yet those words are still before us today. They speak about fidelity to the truth and the person who is Truth. They speak of the tragedies that people of all times and ages bring on themselves by actions guided only by expediency and self-interest. They speak of a God who tries to use even tragedy and disaster to recall his erring children to himself. And they speak of a loving God who will not let his good designs be twisted into meaninglessness. He himself will inaugurate a new covenant that will bind people and God together forever.

SUGGESTIONS FOR REFLECTION

1. "As usual, as the relationship of the people with their God decayed, so did the way the people treated each other." Do you agree with this statement? How does it pertain to life in 20th century America?

2. Compare the call of Jeremiah (Jer.1.4-14) with that of Isaiah (Is. 6.1-13). Who did the calling? How did the prophet respond? What was the message of each to be? Was each one successful?

3. Why is "I will not serve" (Jer. 2.20) seen to represent the classic stance of sinfulness? When else in Scripture or tradition have you heard it?

4. Six centuries later Jesus was to see his relationship to Yahweh as son to "Father." Do you think he might have

been helped to come to this insight from reading and praying Jeremiah 3? What effect did it have on his own prayer style?

5. Oppression and all sorts of injustice against the weak and poor were the cause of Jeremiah's denunciations against the Temple-goers. Who are today's "weak and poor" ones whom Church-goers tend to overlook and ignore rather than assist?

6. The prophet's personal lifestyle was used by Yahweh to be a sign that spoke his message to the nation. Can you suggest any other occasions in history or contemporary times when personal lifestyle spoke a prophetic message? How does your own personal lifestyle speak a prophetic message to this generation? To yourself?

7. Recall and list some of the sufferings of the prophet Jeremiah's life and vocation. In the face of them, what enabled him to go on speaking the word of the Lord? Was he free to have rejected his call? Can the same sufferings be expected by a prophet today? Is the same reassurance of help available today?

8. Why are the psalms helpful prayers for a prophet in distress? Which ones have helped you?

9. Both true and false prophets can sound very persuasive. Both are present around us today. What criterion does Jeremiah offer for our decision-making regarding which to follow? (Jer. 27, 28).

10. In the Eucharistic Prayer IV of the Mass the priest prays to God, "Again and again you offered a covenant to man, and through the prophets taught him to hope for salvation." How do the life and history of Jeremiah prove this? Locate verses from the book of Jeremiah that shed light on this prayer.

11. How can Jeremiah's life of "sustained grief and sorrow" speak a powerful message to the person of faith today? What is his most meaningful message for you?

12. In general, what kind of God does Jeremiah's prophecy depict?

CHAPTER VII

EZEKIEL AND THE AWESOME GOD WHO BRINGS LIFE FROM DEATH

EZEKIEL AND HIS TIMES

Ezekiel is spokesman for Yahweh through the wrenching period of the destruction of the kingdom of Judah and the early years of the Exile. A sketchy outline of his life emerges from the book that bears his name. Ezekiel was a priest from Jerusalem. He was probably one of those taken into exile in Babylonia in the first deportation of 597. In Babylonia, he began his prophetic ministry in 593, and there he remained sharing the fate of the other deportees. His wife died shortly before or during the 587 siege of Jerusalem. The last datable reference in the book is 571 (29.17).

EZEKIEL'S CALL

Please read: 1.1–3.15

Because of the vivid, sometimes bizarre imagery, reading Ezekiel requires some patience.

There are two aspects to Ezekiel's call. One focus is on the *word* (1.2-3; 1.28b–3.11). Ezekiel describes hearing a voice that tells him to remind the Israelites of their rebellion and infidelity. He then sees a vision of a hand holding a scroll on which a message is written. He is commanded to eat the scroll.

The point of this incident is that Ezekiel makes the word of Yahweh his own in a very intimate way. He finds the taste of what he has eaten very sweet. It is Yahweh's good word even if it proposes a bitter and tragic lesson for Israel.

A second focus is on a *vision* (1.1; 1.4-28a; 3.12-15). Ezekiel sees four creatures whose features and characteristics make them inhabitants of a mythological divine world. With these creatures is a complicated wheeled contraption. I deliberately refrain from trying to explain the details of these creatures and the vehicle. Too much remains obscure. The important point is that all details emphasize the fact that Yahweh is present. His mysterious presence pervades the atmosphere. In 3.12-15, this striking but really unimaginable collection of symbols is depicted as rising from its place and flying off.

The *word* account stresses Ezekiel's call to preach the traditional prophetic message of popular rebelliousness against Yahweh and the punishment it deserves.

The *vision* account stresses Ezekiel's call to preach the message of the greatness and mobility of Yahweh. The exiles in Babylonia, Ezekiel included, need not feel abandoned. Yahweh can, and will, be among them.

THE DEFILEMENT OF THE TEMPLE

Please read: 8.3-15; 9.1-11; 10.18-19; 11.22-23

With a series of snap-shot-like scenes, Ezekiel reveals the people as so depraved that pagan gods are being worshiped even in Yahweh's Temple in Jerusalem. He is taken on a tour, in imagination, of the Temple.

First, he sees the "statue of jealousy," a statue or painted slab representing some pagan god or goddess, possibly

Ashtart, a goddess of fertility (8.3-6). Next, in 8.7-12, he visits another part of the Temple decorated with pictures and idols of gods in the forms of snakes and animals. Before these, some of the Israelite leaders are burning incense. In still another place (8.14-15), Ezekiel observes women "weeping for Tammuz." Tammuz was a Babylonian god associated with the cycles of nature. In the fall, when all nature seemed dead, Tammuz was believed to have descended into the underworld. His absence was reflected in the death and stillness in nature. There was ritual mourning for the god because the barrenness of nature was keenly felt.

This unspeakable desecration of Yahweh's Temple can only bring disaster (9.1-11). Six destroyers come into the city. With them is a scribe or secretary. This individual is to go through the city to mark those who do not take part in false worship. Those who are guilty of infidelity will be punished. Innocent individuals will be spared from the tragedy to come.

In the final scene, the creatures and the wheel familiar from the call of Ezekiel make their appearance. Once again, these symbols of Yahweh's presence leave the Temple. In the call narrative, Yahweh's leaving the Temple was a sign of consolation to the exiles. Yahweh could and would be with them even if they were far from their Temple and homeland.

Here, Yahweh's departure is a sign of his displeasure with what is going on in the Temple. The people have defiled the place of his presence with their worship of gods who are nothing. Yahweh, the loving God, who freely chose to be with his people, now freely chooses to abandon the place of his special presence.

THE SINS OF JERUSALEM

Please read: 22.1-31

This chapter summarizes Yahweh's indictment of his people presented through Ezekiel. It is a sordid list of charges. Idolatry. Oppression of the poor and helpless. Desecration of the sabbath. False witness. Sexual abuses. Bribery and usury. Because of all these sins, the judgment of Yahweh will descend.

A HISTORY OF INFIDELITY: TWO SISTERS

Please read: 23.1-49

Ezekiel tells a story of two sisters named Oholah and Oholibah. Oholah represents the northern kingdom and Oholibah the southern kingdom. Both names literally have the word, "tent," as their root and probably refer to Yahweh's "tent" or presence in Samaria and Jerusalem.

Ezekiel tells their story with an explicitness that could offend delicacy.

For the most part, the prophets had seen the time of the Exodus and wandering in the wilderness as an ideal period during which Israel was faithful to Yahweh. Ezekiel rejects this "good old days" nostalgia. From his point of view, Israel was corrupt even from its very origins in Egypt. The two sisters, the two kingdoms, are portrayed as prostitutes always lusting after foreign gods and foreign countries.

Despite the disaster that had fallen on the northern kingdom in 721, the southern kingdom of Judah had learned nothing. The lustful surviving sister continued her lusting. There is no solution except for this sister also to taste the penalty for adultery.

FALSE PROPHETS OF PEACE

Please read: 13.1-16

The conflict with other "prophets" once more emerges. The accusation of Ezekiel is that there are many who are claiming to speak in the name of Yahweh. The message they proclaim is "Peace," "All will be well."

But this is not what Yahweh wishes preached at this time. This is not what the people need to hear. What they need to hear is the strong and challenging call to reform their lives and their relationship with Yahweh. Because the "prophets" fail in their responsibility, they leave the people defenseless against the terror of the future.

EZEKIEL AND SIGNS

Please read: 4.1-3; 5.1-4; 12.1-7; 24.15-23

The ministry of Ezekiel is portrayed as especially characterized by the number of signs, actions meant to illustrate and emphasize his word. There are no less than twelve recounted.

In 4.1-3, Ezekiel is commanded to make a kind of model of Jerusalem surrounded by the instruments of siege: tower, battering rams, enemy camps. This model represents what will happen to Jerusalem.

Again, in 5.1-4, Ezekiel is told to shave his hair and beard. One third of the hair is to burned within the city, one third to be scattered around the city and struck with a sword, and the final third thrown into the wind while he strikes at it with a sword. This gesture says all that has to be said about the fate of Jerusalem. Many will die in the fall of the city. Others will flee in all directions with their enemies in pursuit. Only a small remnant will survive.

It is not clear that Ezekiel actually carried out these symbolic actions. The description of the actions was enough to make the point. However, in 24.15-23 an incident in Ezekiel's life carries a heavy burden of message. Ezekiel's wife dies. In this personal tragedy, he goes through none of the usual mourning rites. He remains silent and apparently insensitive to his loss. The surprised people who observe his behavior ask him to explain.

Ezekiel responds. His insensitivity to the loss of his wife is a sign of Yahweh's insensitivity to the loss of Jerusalem and its faithless people. It is pointless for the people to perform the rites of mourning bewailing the loss of Jerusalem. Her destruction is no more than she has merited by infidelity. It should be said that this sign cost Ezekiel great pain. Unlike the people, his wife had not been unfaithful. In v. 16, she is called "the delight of your eyes."

THE CHALLENGE TO THE INDIVIDUAL

Please read: 18

To explain the tragedies that have beset them, some people are resorting to a proverb. "Fathers have eaten green grapes, thus their children's teeth are on edge." They cannot see what they have done wrong to deserve invasion and exile. As they perceive the situation, the evil is somebody else's fault. With a self-righteousness that may or may not be justified, they do not find anything in their own conduct deserving of such heavy-handed retribution. They complain that they are being made to suffer the penalty for the sins of people who lived before them.

Ezekiel insists that each person is important before God. Yahweh knows the good and the evil that each person does. Good and evil will receive what they deserve.

Furthermore, no one is locked into one way of life. If the person who has been doing evil recognizes the error and turns once again to a life of integrity, Yahweh rejoices. On the other hand, the virtuous person must be careful about that virtue. It is always possible to do wrong and come under judgment.

The last two verses of this chapter say it well. "Cast away from you all the crimes you have committed, and make for yourselves a new heart and a new spirit. Why should you die, O house of Israel? For I have no pleasure in the death of anyone who dies, says the Lord GOD. Return and live!"

A NEW BEGINNING

Please read: 37.1-14

Like Jeremiah, Ezekiel finds that the history of his people drives him to the conclusion that they are radically corrupt. We have already seen this in Chapter 23 where Ezekiel, contrary to what the other prophets say, describes the people as unfaithful to Yahweh even in the days of the Exodus. This charge of corruption is stressed in other passages such as 20.1-31.

However, this conclusion, the bitter fruit of experience, does not drive Ezekiel to despair any more than it did Jeremiah. Rather, with great hope, Ezekiel affirms the continuing goodness of Yahweh toward his people.

Their situation now is like death in its starkest form. Ezekiel imagines a vast plain covered with the bones of dead men. Yahweh asks an unusual question. "Can these bones come to life?"

The question is unusual because a substantial belief in an afterlife has not yet developed in Israel, no less a belief in the resurrection of the body.

At Yahweh's command, Ezekiel orders the bones to be formed into bodies and to be filled again with life. The dead bones obey and live again.

The vision is not about resurrection from the dead but about the fate of Israel. At that moment, the future of Israel looked as promising as a plain full of dry bones. But what is impossible to men is not impossible to God. At his command, Israel will once again become a people.

"I will put my spirit in you that you may live, and I will settle you upon your land; thus you shall know that I am the LORD. I have promised, and I will do it, says the LORD." Despite the reality of sin, despite the apparent hopelessness of their situation, God has not abandoned his people. He will once more give them life.

THE NEW COVENANT

Please read: 36.22-32; 37.21-28

Ezekiel, like Jeremiah, envisions a new relationship between Yahweh and his people.

The old covenant failed. The way of life it called for in response to Yahweh's goodness proved beyond the capabilities of the people. Now Yahweh would act again, not in giving rules and regulations, no matter how good, but in breathing an interior power into people to enable them to live as true sons of God. He would "give . . . a new heart and place a new spirit within you, taking from your bodies your stony hearts and giving you natural hearts. I will put my spirit within you and make you live by my statutes" (36.26-27). "I will make with them a covenant of peace; it shall be an everlasting covenant with them . . . I will be their God, and they shall be my people" (37.26-27). Through this radical new situation, all will come to recognize the goodness and power of the holy God of Israel.

EZEKIEL AND THE NEW TEMPLE

Chapters 40–48 have a long, sometimes tedious, description of a rebuilt Temple in Jerusalem. It is not important to try to visualize the Temple and city. Many of the details are not clear even as Ezekiel describes them. Furthermore, the description represents a kind of utopia, an ideal temple in an ideal land in an ideal situation. Like all such descriptions, the importance does not lie with an accurate understanding of the architectural arrangements.

A key passage in this long description is 43.1-9. Earlier in his prophetic ministry, Ezekiel envisioned the holy and transcendent God leaving his Temple in Jerusalem. Yahweh was not imprisoned in or limited to the Temple. He was beyond any efforts to contain him in one place or one situation. He could go with his people into exile in Babylonia. He could also withdraw his presence because of the sinfulness with which his people defiled his special place.

As Ezekiel looks to the future, he sees a situation of an ideal Jerusalem and an ideal Temple. In this reformed and rebuilt land lasting goodness and fidelity to Yahweh would flourish. The new situation would be that Yahweh would "dwell in their midst forever" (43.9).

As Ezekiel imagines the ideal future of Israel, he sees a stream flowing from the Temple toward the East (47. 1-12). As the stream moves away from the Temple, it becomes deeper and deeper. On its banks, all kinds of trees grow. The water is wonderfully fresh and filled with fish. Wherever it flows, living things prosper and thrive.

What Ezekiel asserts here is that when Yahweh is truly and permanently present in that hoped-for future, his presence will mean fertility and prosperity for the land also. In the Old Testament, the fate of people and the fate of nature are intimately tied together. The new presence of Yahweh among his people, the new fidelity on their part, bring a new splendor to the rest of creation.

EZEKIEL AS THE "SON OF MAN"

Again and again, Ezekiel, is addressed by Yahweh as "Son of man" (cf. 2.1; 3.1; 3.17; 4.1; 6.1, etc.). Lest the association of this term with Jesus in the Gospels cause some confusion, we might note its meaning in the book of Ezekiel.

"Son of" in Hebrew simply designates a person as a member of a certain group. Thus, "son of man" means someone who is a man.

What the term especially emphasizes here is the fact that man is less than nothing before the greatness and wonder of the holy God. Ezekiel, in the awesome presence of God, is reminded of his own humanity and frailty. At the same time, the use of the expression emphasizes the power of Yahweh in another way. He is able to use even his fragile creature to accomplish his purposes in the world.

THE MESSAGE OF EZEKIEL

Ezekiel exercises his prophetic ministry through years of tragedy and disaster for Judah and Jerusalem. His style, filled with strange visions and images, is not always easy to follow. Unlike most of the oracles of the other prophets, much of what he said is preserved not in poetic form but in sometimes very complex prose. Yet the thrust of his preaching is clear enough.

Jerusalem and Judah have sinned and so have driven away from themselves the saving presence of the living God. His absence will spell disaster. In fact, the whole history of Israel from its very beginnings in the Exodus is tainted with sin and infidelity. Since then, the situation has gotten worse.

But in the face of this radical experience of sinfulness, there is an even more radical expression of hope. God has not abandoned his people. He calls them to a new, deep and lasting relationship with him that is so different from the way things were that it can only be understood as a different covenant and likened to a plain full of dead bones coming to life or to a newly built Temple in Jerusalem.

Yahweh will bring all this about because he will have both his own people and the nations of the world recognize that he is Yahweh, the living, saving, holy God of Israel.

SUGGESTIONS FOR REFLECTION

1. The Word of God has been described in many images in the Scriptures as a two-edged sword, a lamp to our feet, a home, etc. Ezekiel sees it as a sweet-tasting scroll to be eaten. If you were to look at your life experience with the Word of God, how would you image or describe it?

2. "The people have defiled Yahweh's presence (in the Temple) with their worship of gods who are nothing." If you consider your own self as a Temple, is Yahweh pleased with the worship of his presence there? Or does Yahweh share his place in your Temple with "worship of gods who are nothing?"

3. Jeremiah had seen the Temple worship as defiled in a different way from that of Ezekiel. Compare and contrast their two views.

4. Yahweh's anger is stirred against his people for their sins in Ezekiel 22; how does that description of the nation compare with headlines in our newspapers and media to-day? Would Ezekiel find food for prophecy in our midst? Do you ever see yourself as an Ezekiel?

5. Sometimes today's prophets use symbolic gestures and actions to make their point—peace marches, Indian and poor peoples rallies, civil rights and non-violent de-monstrations, etc. How do such visual means flow direct-ly from the prophetic tradition and style of Ezekiel?

6. At times parents feel a heavy burden of responsibility for the choices and decisions of their children, even though they did everything possible through example and teaching to educate them in God's ways. How does the word of Ezekiel in chapter 18 relieve minds and hearts weighed down by this burden?

7. Though Ezekiel's vision of the valley of dry bones re-flected the condition of the whole nation of Israel, most of us have at times felt personally as though "our bones are dried up, our hope is lost." Recall a time in your life when such a condition prevailed, and you received an un-expected grace of new spirit, new life, an opening of your "grave" from which the Lord helped you to rise.

8. After reading chapters 36 and 37, make a list of ad-jectives that could describe Yahweh God. What do these imply about how the people should respond in a covenant relationship?

9. If you could have a "new heart," a "new spirit," what about you would change? Has it ever happened to you? Think of one person in your life to whom you would like to give a new heart or new spirit, and take several moments to bring this person in prayer before the Lord, requesting

it. Take a tangible step yourself to do something that might bring newness to that person.

10. Ezekiel's bizarre imagery is a characteristic of style that distinguishes his word from the other prophets. Review his imagery in his visions—the presence of Yahweh, the Temple, and the valley of dry bones.

11. How does Ezekiel underline the awesomeness of God in contrast to the frailty of man?

CHAPTER VIII

SECOND ISAIAH AND THE CONSOLATION OF GOD

"Second Isaiah" is surely an unusual name for anyone. Yet this is the name used to refer to the person responsible for chapters 40–55 of the book of Isaiah. We use this title (or sometimes "Deutero-Isaiah" which means the same thing but substitutes the Greek word for "second") because the identity of the one who left us the prophetic message in these chapters is not known.

The chapters have been included with the prophetic utterances of the prophet Isaiah, about whom we read earlier. However, it is clear that these sayings are about 150 years later than the oracles of Isaiah. Careful study shows that the historical situation in Second Isaiah is very different from that in Isaiah. Jerusalem and Judah are not being threatened with destruction and exile for their infidelity. The punishment has already taken place. Second Isaiah offers hope and consolation to those in exile. Further, there are differences in style and language that strongly suggest two different authors for chapters 1–39 and 40–55.

THE CALL OF SECOND ISAIAH

Please read: 40.1-11

This anonymous spokesman for Yahweh understands his mission in terms of "comforting" the people. From the grief and trouble in which they now dwell will come the lasting joy and peace of God.

Twice, in 597 and again in much larger numbers in 587, people from Jersualem and Judah had been brought to Babylonia as exiles. Generally the people thus uprooted were those who were better educated and of leadership caliber. These were the ones who might make trouble for their Babylonian conquerors and stir up rebellion if they were left on their home ground. They were kept in much better control if they were a minority in the land of their overlords than if they were allowed to live unsupervised at some distance from their masters.

Apparently the lot of the exiles was not excessively burdensome. They engaged in business. They farmed. They established families. They were able to maintain their identity.

However, their sense of loss did not die. They knew that they were far from their homeland. They knew that the Temple of their God had been destroyed. Second Isaiah emerges from this group some time about the year 550 B.C., when the exile has been a reality for a whole generation.

The first scene in Second Isaiah's call is most likely to be understood as the heavenly court. God speaks. "Comfort, give comfort to my people." Some prophets before the exile had rejected the name, "Yahweh's people" for Israel because of its infidelity. Now, once more, God calls the humbled exiles, "my people." The heavenly court is commanded to "speak to the heart" of Jerusalem. The time of punishment, so well deserved because of the history of sinfulness, is finished.

When Eastern kings visited the distant parts of their kingdoms, the road system was repaired so that the royal chariot could make speed. Second Isaiah hears a heavenly voice commanding the beings around Yahweh to prepare on earth for God to reveal his power. Since the route from Babylonia to Judah was across the desert, the return of the exiles, to be brought about by God, is envisioned as taking place along a vast highway across the wilderness.

With v. 6, Second Isaiah is brought into the scene. He is called to recognize the greatness of Yahweh. All mankind and the glories of mankind pass away. They are like the grass of the field. But the word of Yahweh lasts forever.

That word stands even in the face of what was the power of Babylon, now in decline. That word is that Yahweh, always good, will bring his people back to their homeland. No passing human forces will be able to stand in the way of his will.

THE NEW EXODUS

Please read: 43.14-21

Yahweh reaffirms the reality of his titles. He is *redeemer,* the savior of his people from their afflictions. He is the *Holy One of Israel* whose power and life stand over against human weakness. (Recall how important this belief was in Isaiah and you have one reason why these chapters are connected to Isaiah 1–39). He is the *creator* of Israel who made this people his by saving acts on their behalf. And he is their *king.* This God is acting again. He is lowering the bars of the gates that lock his people in the prison of Babylon.

Yahweh showed the kind of God he is when he liberated his people from slavery in Egypt. He led this people to liberty through the Sea. When Egypt's army followed, it met disaster. This is the God that Israel has been taught about and remembers.

Now Israel is told that something even greater is to happen. Jeremiah expressed what Yahweh would do in terms of a "new covenant." This would be more wonderful than the "old" because it would be a force in human hearts and would last forever, bringing Yahweh's peace. Second Isaiah expresses Yahweh's action in terms of a new Exodus.

What Yahweh did in the past will be as nothing compared to what he is about to do now. He will lead his people in a new march to liberation. In the wilderness through which the returning columns must journey, Yahweh will prepare a path and will tame even the wild animals and the inhospitable land. Yahweh never forgets his people.

CYRUS AS YAHWEH'S INSTRUMENT

Please read: 45.1-13

Around the middle of the sixth century B.C., a new force emerged in the area dominated by Babylon. This was Cyrus the Persian and his armies. His power spread irresistibly over the lands once under the control of Babylon. Cyrus proved to be not only a conqueror but an enlightened ruler. He showed great toleration and concern for the beliefs of those under his rule.

As the reports of Cyrus' exploits and conquests buzz through Babylon, Second Isaiah makes a startling announcement. Yahweh is responsible for the success of Cyrus. Cyrus is called Yahweh's *messiah,* which is the Hebrew word for anointed. This term had been reserved for the kings of Judah and designated them as filled with the power of Yahweh to do his work.

With a grand vision that passes beyond national boundaries, Second Isaiah sees that Yahweh controls the fate and destiny of all nations and can use any and all to accomplish his purposes. The foreigner, Cyrus, can serve Yahweh's plan. Yahweh is the one who cracks open the defenses of the cities that Cyrus captures. This is true even if Yahweh says to Cyrus, "you knew me not."

The fact that Yahweh had chosen such a foreigner to do his work was not easy for his own people to accept. In vv. 9-13, Second Isaiah speaks to their feelings. Yahweh's free creative act for his people is no more open to question by them than clay can ask the one who shapes it, "What are you doing?" His people can no more question his creative action than they question the creative activity of father and mother.

Yahweh, the creator, never ceases in his work of creation. His creative activity is directed not simply toward a "place," but also the quality of the "place." He intends a universe marked with peace, justice and harmony. Connected with this creative act in its long range implications is the return of the exiles to Jerusalem. Yahweh will accomplish this through Cyrus the foreigner.

YAHWEH THE ONLY GOD

Please read: 45.1-8; 44.6-8; 45.20-25

It is in Second Isaiah that we get the first statements that Yahweh is the *only* God.

"I am the LORD and there is no other,
there is no God besides me."

This is not to say that Israel believed in and worshiped other gods until the middle of the sixth century B.C. From the time of the Exodus, Israel had been told that the only God who counted was Yahweh. Yahweh was the God who controlled Israel's history and the history of the lands around it. Now that belief with all its implications finds clear, vigorous expression.

ISRAEL HAS STILL NOT LEARNED

Please read: 42.18-25

Not all of what Second Isaiah has to say is hope and consolation. Here Israel is called "deaf" and "blind." The reason is that Israel has not yet learned the lesson of its history. Despite all that has happened, the people do not understand. They do not appreciate that Yahweh is present in what has been going on. In the afflictions that struck them, he reminded them of their sinfulness and called them to repentance. Somehow this lesson has been lost. But they must learn. Their role as Yahweh's servant, as a people entrusted with a mission to the world, is in danger if they do not truly know the God they serve.

THE FATE OF BABYLON

Please read: 47.1-15

Yahweh controls history. Such is the belief of those who professed Yahweh as their God. Yahweh had in the past used the foreign power, Babylon, to turn the people from their infidelity to him. Babylon had captured and devastated the homeland of Yahweh's people.

But now, Babylon, portrayed as a young woman, must collect the wages it has been storing up. Babylon will be defeated and humiliated. Its crime? The fact that it did not realize its place in history, in a plan conceived by Yahweh. Babylon imagined, "I shall remain always a sovereign mistress forever!" It was blind to its mortality as compared to Yahweh, the Holy One of Israel.

Nothing. Not its might, not its magicians and sorcerers, certainly not its lifeless gods, can save it.

THE SERVANT OF YAHWEH

Within chapters 40–55 are four passages of special importance. These passages, 42.1-4; 49.1-6; 50.4-9a; 52.13–53.12, are all about the "servant of Yahweh."

The word "servant" has a long and honorable history in the Old Testament. Applied to the servant of a king, the word suggests honor and obedience to the king. The servant exercises the authority of the king in the king's name. At the same time, the servant is absolutely and totally obedient to his royal master. He is able to be trusted by the one he serves.

In the Old Testament, Abraham, Jacob, Moses and David, among others, are designated as servants of Yahweh or God. (The Hebrew word for servant is *ebed*). Any loyal follower of Yahweh could be called his servant. However, the servant of Yahweh was especially one designated to play a significant role in God's plan. In fact, the people, Israel, is designated as "servant" several times in Second Isaiah, e.g., in 41.8; 44.1.

The four passages mentioned above seem to go beyond the usual import of servant.

THE FIRST SERVANT SONG

Please read: 42.1-4

Here Yahweh speaks. He introduces the servant as a kind of court official. Possibly the scene envisioned is Yahweh introducing the servant to his heavenly court.

The servant has a special mission, to bring justice, i.e., the filling of all life and worship with the presence of Yahweh. For this role, Yahweh will give his own power and strength to his servant.

Even with his tremendously important role, the servant will not imitate the brute power and pompous posturing of other great authorities. He will be mild and gentle, considerate of the weak and helpless. His mission is not narrow and limited. The truth and peace he brings is for all nations.

THE SECOND SERVANT SONG

Please read: 49.1-6

Now the speaker is the servant himself. He describes his call. In words reminiscent of Jeremiah, he speaks of his call from birth. However, Yahweh chose to keep him "concealed" and "hidden" until it was time for him to undertake his mission.

V. 4 seems to indicate that this person, whose role is depicted as that of a prophet, as one speaking in Yahweh's name, had first met rejection in his preaching. But now the servant realizes his task must be taken up again. He has a glorious mission, "to restore the survivors of Israel." But even beyond this, by fulfilling his mission, the servant will become
"a light to the nations,
that my salvation may reach to the ends of the earth."

THE THIRD SERVANT SONG

Please read: 50.4-9

Once again the servant speaks. And once again he presents himself in terms of a prophet. Yahweh has given him a "well-trained tongue" that he may voice encouragement to the weary exiles. The presence of Yahweh to his servant is constant.

But, for reasons not at all clear, the servant, in carrying out his mission, meets not just opposition or contradiction but persecution. He refers to himself as beaten and mocked. Despite this, he is determined to continue. He knows that Yahweh is with him. Yahweh has sent him on his mission and will be with him.

THE FOURTH SERVANT SONG

Please read: 52.13–53.12

In 52.13-15 and 53.11-12, Yahweh would seem to be the speaker. Between the two statements of Yahweh, either Israel or the people of the nations of the world seem to be speaking.

The servant is again introduced by Yahweh. A promise is made that he will be exalted, and this despite the fact that those seeing him would be shocked by his suffering-marred appearance. Other speakers then reflect on the servant and the suffering and rejection he has undergone.

Then comes the realization that what the servant underwent was for the benefit of all. In some way, what he did would have far-reaching effects. His path of suffering led even to the depths of death, and to a burial in dishonor.

The poem ends with Yahweh once again speaking of the servant. He affirms that the sufferings of the servant are acts of salvation for the sins of others.

WHO WAS THE SERVANT?

As we read the Servant Songs, the "biography" of the servant that seems to emerge is that of a prophet who comes to speak in the name of Yahweh. The prophet, faithful to his mission, preaches the coming salvation of Yahweh for Israel and all nations. For some reason, he encounters first opposition and then outright persecution. This persecution reaches its climax in the suffering and death of the servant.

But Yahweh has the last word. The servant, even in suffering, fulfills his mission. His agony, accepted though he does not deserve it, works the cleansing from sin for others.

Over the centuries, those, both Christian and Jewish, who have studied, meditated on and prayed these poems, have tried to discover who the servant might be. Theories without end have been proposed.

The servant is the prophet, Second Isaiah, himself.
The servant is a disciple of Second Isaiah.
The servant is the people, Israel.
The servant is a faithful core of Israel.

Perhaps the best interpretation is that which tries to include several possibilities. Second Isaiah begins by describing the role of Israel in saving the nations in terms of his own experience and prophetic vocation. However, as his understanding of the role of Yahweh's servant grows and deepens, he is led to affirm a more and more exalted vocation for the servant. This vocation of the servant can have no fulfillment except in some special individual in God's future.

Thus, there is a coming together of the role of the prophet himself, the role he understands for Israel, and the recognition that the mission to the world that he foresees will not be fulfilled until the time when Yahweh intervenes in some special way.

The early Christians understood these passages as a description of the role of Jesus, as do we. The fourth song especially was interpreted as a prophecy of his suffering and death.

THE MESSAGE OF SECOND ISAIAH

The unknown prophet who, for want of a better name, is called Second Isaiah offers a message of hope.

Hope is in the air. The Persian king, Cyrus, is on the march. He has shown himself an enlightened and broad-minded ruler, generous to captives. The once fearsome might of Babylon that holds captive the exiles from Judah is tottering. Second Isaiah calls his fellow exiles to recognize the hand of Yahweh in what is happening. Yahweh is working through this foreign king to bring them home. Believing Israel has kept alive its faith in the God who liberated its ancestors from Egypt. Now something new and greater is stirring. Yahweh will perform a new Exodus and liberate his people from captivity. The one who created the world is loosing his creative force to make a new people.

While Second Isaiah does not forget the sins, past and present, of the people, his vocation is to offer the people the future Yahweh holds out to them. And through the work of the servant, Yahweh's salvation will spread even to the other nations of the world.

SUGGESTIONS FOR REFLECTION

1. Explain why scholars think that chapters 40-55 may have been written by a different author from chapters 1–39 in the book of Isaiah.

2. Trace the history of the people in "Second Isaiah," from its background in the book of Jeremiah, and continuing through that of Ezekiel. Make a time line to show the movements of history.

3. Re-read chapter 40.1-11 to note ways in which Jesus might have been inspired by it as he went about his public mission.

4. In chapter 40.8 we learn another quality that describes the word of God, namely, eternal. How does this insight differ from insights about the word in Jeremiah and Ezekiel?

5. Re-read the book of Exodus, chapters 14 through 17, to review for yourself the details of the Lord's kindness in saving his people from the Egyptians, and to appreciate better the parallel of a "New Exodus" from Babylon which Isaiah describes in chapter 43.14-21. How is the Lord doing "something new,' bringing about a new exodus from slavery and captivity in your life today?

6. Yahweh uses an unexpected person, the foreigner, Cyrus, to bring about the liberation of his own captive people. The Lord is ultimately behind all history. How has he acted through something or someone unexpected in your life to bring you out of desolation and captivity into consolation and freedom? Did you at first recognize and welcome his hand in it, or did you at first tend, like the Israelites, to reject it as "alien," "foreign?"

7. Israel's "role as Yahweh's servant, as a people entrusted with a mission to the world, is in danger if they do not truly know the God they serve." How does this same danger exist among us Christians because of our deafness and blindness which at times prevent us from *knowing* the ways of the God we serve?

8. Yahweh's people thought he had abandoned them in exile. In chapter 47, his angry address to Babylon, he promised to come to the rescue of his own. Recall a

time in your life when although you felt like the Israelites, that he had forgotten you, he ultimately came to your rescue.

9. Since pride, arrogance, and oppression of the weak are sins against which Yahweh is always angered, Isaiah's Yahweh shows no partiality in punishment for them. Compare how his threats to sinful Babylon resemble those he has previously made against sinful Israel. Which other prophets had shown Yahweh to be Lord, not only of the Israelites, but of all peoples and history?

10. Read through the "Servant Songs" and reflect on how the servant might be seen as the people, or the faithful core, Israel?

11. The "Servant Songs" gradually reveal deeper and deeper understanding of the meaning of a prophet's life. How has your own revelation of the meaning of life changed and deepened with your growing and maturing?

12. Read the "Servant Songs" again and select from them one verse or one idea that speaks to you today with meaning for the human condition. Share your insight with another person.

13. Second Isaiah is a prophet of hope. Which segment of his message could be applied with the most hope for our times as you look at the world today?

CHAPTER IX

THE PROPHETS: SUMMING UP

Our survey of the prophets has demonstrated that they were convinced that they spoke for God. Their message was often harsh. The sins of the people were calling down on them fitting retribution. The people had chosen to put their trust in more up-to-date gods, in wealth and power, in the political forces of their day. They would learn through bitter experience that, in the long run, one cannot build life on these. Because the rich and powerful oppressed the poor and helpless, the justice of God would pursue them.

But at issue is not vengeance and retribution. Behind the prophetic denunciation is the call to return to Yahweh. Yahweh is the husband of his people, their father, the one bound to them in covenant. Only in him does their existence have meaning and purpose.

When the prophetic call to conversion went unheeded, prophetic voices grew more and more strident. Finally, at the end of a long history, there is the anguished accusation that the people are corrupt and perverse at their very core.

Even this is not the end. The God who loves and calls his people to him will transform even this radical perversity. He has never stopped being their God. They will once again become his people.

THE TRUTH OF THE PROPHETS

We have come to know in some detail prophets whose preaching spanned two centuries, from 750 to 550 B.C. They have been different kinds of men.

Amos, a shepherd shocked by pervasive inhumanity, by the contrast between riches and poverty in the cities of the north and disgusted by the emptiness of the never-ending religious observances.

Hosea, a betrayed husband, whose experience threw into bold relief the infidelity of Israel and the love of God.

Isaiah, a man at home in the royal court and Temple, who stood in awe of the wonderful otherness of God and in horror of the way his people betrayed their past, present and future by pinning their hopes on forces that were as nothing compared to their God.

Jeremiah, tormented by his mission to condemn and challenge, rejected by his own family and those he desperately tried to reach, a witness to the final tragedy of his people.

Ezekiel, a priest who shared the lot of his exiled countrymen, who knew the enormity of their sin but also the boundlessness of God's mercy.

Second Isaiah, a man unknown who offered to the exiles the hope of return and restoration.

Each of these men believed that he spoke for God. But most of those who heard them obviously did not share that belief. The prophets were ignored, rejected, ridiculed, told to be silent, persecuted.

Why could they not convince others of the truth of what they were saying? To put it another way, how could those who heard them know they were speaking the truth? After all, history has shown again and again that it is not hard for one to become deluded into believing that he or she has a divine message. Witness the tragedy of Jonestown, Guyana.

Just what guarantee is there that someone claiming to be a prophet is really speaking for God and not from the desire for notoriety, or from greed for personal gain, or from madness, or from simple misunderstanding?

The prophets whose words are in the Old Testament were proven to be true by the events of history. The Jews in exile searched out and put together the collections of sayings of the prophets that had been preserved by their faithful followers. The prophetic teaching was the key to understanding why Israel was in exile and the stimulus for persevering hope in God.

Yet this criterion is surely not very helpful at the moment that the prophet speaks. The listener who heard Hananiah, accepted as a prophet, proclaim that Yahweh would soon end the exile, and Jeremiah, also claiming to be a prophet, contradict him (Jeremiah 28) would be hard pressed to know how to respond if he had to wait for history to show which was correct.

Jeremiah, in that same chapter, claims that a criterion for the truth of the prophet is whether he speaks prosperity or woe. The prophet traditionally, according to Jeremiah, preaches disaster. A prophet who preaches that all is well is suspect (Jeremiah 28.8-9). Ezekiel 13.1-16 seems to take for granted the same rule of thumb.

According to this standard, the basic function of a prophet is to warn, to call people from infidelity and sinfulness, to turn them once again to God and his ways. Prophets like

Second Isaiah are an exception to this rule, although he also called the Jews to deeper faith and fidelity.

Certainly one sign of the true prophet is conformity with the best tradition of belief in Yahweh. The prophet's message has authentic tone when heard against the background of Israel's faith and rings true in the heart of one trying to live that faith.

Of course, none of these criteria is fool-proof. Ultimately it is God himself who must draw from the heart of the believer the conviction that the word heard is truly his.

By now all kinds of questions must have been triggered. Are there prophets today? How can we know whether there are? How can we know who they are, if they do exist? What is the relation between the prophet and the "institutional" church?

But these are questions that must be left for answers to the Spirit-guided life and experience of the Christian community today. We search for the answers in company with the noblest hearts in Israel who have gone before us.

SUGGESTIONS FOR FURTHER READING

B. W. Anderson. *Understanding the Old Testament.* 3rd ed. Englewood Cliffs, N.J.: Prentice-Hall, 1975.

G. von Rad. *The Message of the Prophets.* N.Y.: Harper and Row, 1972.

The Liturgical Press, Collegeville, Minn., publishes the *Old Testament Reading Guide.* This inexpensive paperback series include the following titles pertinent to this book:

Introduction to the Prophetical Books of the Old Testament
Amos, Hosea, Micah
Isaiah 1-39
Jeremiah, Baruch
Ezekiel
Zephaniah, Nahum, Habakkuk, Lamentations, Obadiah
Isaiah 40-66
Haggai, Zechariah, Malachi, Joel

The following are important, more advanced reference works containing commentaries on all the Books of the Bible.

R. Brown, (ed.) *The Jerome Biblical Commentary.* Englewood Cliffs, N.J.: Prentice-Hall, 1968.

R. Fuller, (ed.) *A New Catholic Commentary on Holy Scripture.* London: Nelson, 1969.

C. Laymon, (ed.) *The Interpreter's One-Volume Commentary on the Bible.* Nashville: Abingdon Press, 1971.